PARENT-BABBLE

Other Books by John Rosemond

The NEW Six-Point Plan for Raising Happy, Healthy Children

The NEW Parent Power!

Ending the Homework Hassle

Making the "Terrible" Twos Terrific!

A Family of Value

Because I Said So!

Teen Proofing

To Spank or Not to Spank

Family-Building

Parenting by the Book

The Diseasing of America's Children (with Dr. Bose Ravenel)

The Well-Behaved Child: Discipline That REALLY Works!

Parent-Babble

How Parents Can Recover from Fifty Years of Bad Expert Advice

JOHN ROSEMOND

Andrews McMeel
Publishing, LLC

Kansas City • Sydney • London

To my good friend and mentor
Dr. Tom Fagan

Andrews McMeel Publishing, LLC
an Andrews McMeel Universal company
1130 Walnut Street, Kansas City, Missouri 64106

www.andrewsmcmeel.com

12 13 14 15 16 RR2 10 9 8 7 6 5 4 3 2 1

ISBN: 978-1-4494-2233-2

Library of Congress Control Number: 2012936734

ATTENTION: SCHOOLS AND BUSINESSES
Andrews McMeel books are available at quantity discounts with bulk purchase for educational, business, or sales promotional use. For information, please e-mail the Andrews McMeel Publishing Special Sales Department:
specialsales@amuniversal.com

ACKNOWLEDGMENTS

Special appreciation to Christine Schillig, my longtime editor at Andrews McMeel Publishing, for believing in my work and helping me become a better writer. Long may you run, Chris.

Many thanks to Kindred Howard, who did much of the research for, and wrote preliminary drafts of, several chapters.

Recognition to Dr. Michael Youssef, pastor and author of *When All the Crosses Are Gone*, for providing the inspiration for much of chapter one.

Gratitude to my good friend and colleague Dr. Don Jacobsen, for reading the first two chapters and cheering me on.

"*I sometimes think the world will either be saved by psychologists, in the broadest sense, or it will not be saved at all.*"

—ABRAHAM MASLOW, HUMANISTIC PSYCHOLOGIST (1908–1970)

"*There is nothing so absurd that some philosopher has not already said it.*"

—MARCUS TILLIUS CICERO (106–43 BC)

CONTENTS

INTRODUCTION

I am a psychologist licensed by the North Carolina Psychology Board, but please don't jump to any conclusions, pro or con. I'm a psychologist by license only. I don't really believe in psychology—the clinical form, that is. For one thing, I cannot find unbiased, compelling evidence to demonstrate that so-called talk therapy—or any other form of psychological therapy, for that matter—has a reasonably high rate of effectiveness. In fact, I've found significant evidence to the contrary, and as a result, I don't have much confidence in my own field of training.

As I have said many times, in many venues, including several previous books, I came to the conclusion some time ago that clinical psychology is a secular religion—an ideology, in other words—that one accepts by faith. It has its doctrine (ever changing), patron saints (e.g., Freud, Skinner, Rogers), supposedly healing rituals, inquisitions for people like me who dare question its prevailing theories and practices, and excommunications. Psychology pretends to be science, when it actually consists of a set of often contradictory philosophical propositions concerning the nature of human beings. Despite the pretense of scientific, research-based underpinnings, the propositions in question are and always have been driven more by professional fad and consensus than solid, objective research. A personal story will illustrate the point.

In 1979, after submitting my qualifications and passing a rigorous exam, I obtained my license from the North Carolina Psychology

Board and immediately went into private practice. By this time, I had been writing my syndicated newspaper column for three years. Over the next ten years or so, as I began to slowly realize that my profession was promoting parenting practices that were creating huge problems for parents, children, families, schools, and society, my column turned in a radical direction. I became more and more outspoken in my disagreements with my profession's party line. As a consequence, my colleagues became more and more discomfited by what I was saying, the advice I was giving parents. After all, I was threatening their raison d'être, not to mention their standards of living.

In a column I wrote in the late 1980s, I had the temerity to tell two parents that if their young child had been seeing a therapist for six months because of behavior problems and the problems weren't getting better and the therapist had yet to recommend any action to the parents, it was time to find another therapist. Reasonable advice, no? Not as far as my licensing board was concerned. They accused me of interfering in a therapist–client relationship. I plead guilty, but I would say that I was interfering in a relationship between an obviously irresponsible therapist and a gullible client. The board threatened to take my license away but ended up only reprimanding me and putting me on probation.

Several years later, I published another column in which, again responding to concerned parents, I said it was unlikely that a twenty-three-month-old child who had been sexually abused on one occasion by a stranger had formed a permanent memory of the incident. My exact words: "In all likelihood, she has no memory of the event, nor will she ever have memory of it."

That was in 1991, when the popularity of so-called recovered memory therapy was peaking. Lots of mental health professionals had jumped on this very lucrative bandwagon. The premise behind this bogus "therapy" (*brainwashing* is a more apt term) was that nearly every emotional problem borne by adult women—irrational fears, anxieties, depression, sexual dysfunctions, you name it—was the result of repressed memories of childhood sexual abuse. The mental health community claimed that these memories—even memories of sexual abuse that had occurred during infancy—could be retrieved from the subconscious mind and dealt with under very unique, controlled therapeutic circumstances, led by a "qualified" professional (i.e., con artist).

Without any objective evidence, but simply because irresponsible (and, in my estimation, sociopathic) therapists encouraged insecure women to develop traumatic "memories," scores of men—fathers, uncles, brothers, longtime family friends—were unjustly accused of being sex abusers. In some cases the accusation was made decades after the supposed event. All over the country, hundreds if not thousands of innocent people had their reputations destroyed. Some even went to prison. Some committed suicide. Parent–child relationships were destroyed, in some cases irretrievably. And many families were permanently devastated. Meanwhile, a good number of therapists, including a good number of psychologists, were making a good amount of money specializing in this disgusting fraud. Hear me clearly: I am not saying that childhood sexual abuse does not occur; I am simply asserting that unbiased research available at the time did not support the idea that permanent memories, even of trauma, can form in the first two to three years of life. There may be rare exceptions, but that is the rule.

The column I wrote, giving reassuring advice to parents who were understandably upset, was threatening to the therapists in question, a number of whom occupied positions of power and prestige in the mental health establishment. A dozen or so newspapers, inundated with complaints, dropped my column, and several of these therapists complained to my licensing board. After a token investigation, the board accused me of violating professional ethics. This time, I had made statements that were not supported by a *consensus* of mental health professionals. Keep in mind that in the fifteenth century, a consensus of educated men in the sciences and religion believed the earth was the center of the universe. In fact, the Catholic Church was burning people at the stake for believing otherwise. In and of itself, consensus is not proof. It is simply proof that lots of people have faith that the proof will be found. In other words, a mere scientific consensus concerning any issue is insufficient and leaves the issue open to debate. Nonetheless, it was clear that my license and reputation hung in the balance.

Despite the fact that several of the most well-known and respected researchers in the field of human memory—how it forms, how it is stored, how it can be recalled—affirmed that I had been correct in saying the little girl was unlikely to remember the one isolated event, my licensing board pressed ahead. Eventually, after nearly two years of expensive negotiations that necessitated the hiring of two lawyers (one of whom had argued before the Supreme Court), we reached a consent agreement in which I was allowed to keep my license.

Mind you, the point of the story is *not* that I am a victim in any sense of the term. My point is that at any given moment, no guarantee exists that any given psychological practice is based on good science. Therapies are not independently validated before they are used. Tests of a new drug are carried out *before* the drug is released to the public, but psychotherapists try out new therapies on paying customers. In that regard, psychology is akin to a house of cards built on ever-shifting ideological sands. If a consensus develops within the profession, research that might contradict that consensus might be largely ignored. That especially applies to any consensus that results in more people seeking therapy.

In the 1980s, for example, psychologists were diagnosing lots of people with multiple personality disorder and developing specific therapies to help people recover from or deal with it. Over the next twenty years, evidence debunking the diagnosis was presented, and it virtually disappeared from the therapeutic landscape. Has anyone so diagnosed been contacted and told that a mistake may have been made? I doubt it.

A more recent example concerns the diagnosis of attention deficit–hyperactivity disorder (ADHD). As pediatrician DuBose Ravenel and I pointed out in *The Diseasing of America's Children* (2008, Thomas Nelson), there is no compelling evidence that this behavioral condition is transmitted genetically, nor is there compelling evidence of faulty brain circuitry or biochemical imbalance. In fact, these notions have been debunked by good science. Nonetheless, psychologists who dispense this diagnosis persist in telling parents that ADHD is transmitted by genes and is the result of faulty "wiring" or a biochemical imbalance. They ignore evidence to the contrary because the evidence doesn't suit their purposes. In short, ADHD is not a valid diagnosis. It is a convenient *construction* that has resulted, once again, in an unprecedented cash flow for mental health professionals. The only explanation for this disconnect between research and practice is that by convincing parents there is something wrong with their children, therapists are able to greatly increase the likelihood these same parents will agree to expensive, potentially never-ending treatments.

Over the past forty to fifty years, psychology has infected American culture and parenting with one bogus notion after another. For example, I'll bet you didn't know that researchers have discovered a strong relationship between high self-esteem and antisocial behavior; many sociopaths and violent criminals are found to have very high self-esteem. You probably believe that high self-esteem is a really good thing. After all, Oprah says it is. So does Dr. Phil. He's a psychologist, by the way. But who do you think had higher self-esteem: Adolf Hitler or Mother Teresa? Joseph Stalin or George Washington?

Did you know that no one has ever proven that behavior modification works on human beings? That's right, no one. B. F. Skinner never proved it, and no one else has either. Nonetheless, a *consensus* of psychologists will tell you that behavior modification works on human beings. Why do they tell you this if it has not been proven? First, most of them have simply accepted the proposition because it was taught in graduate school and postgraduate seminars. They don't understand that behavior modification *theory* means what it says: It's a theory, not a fact. Second, many of them don't know what else to recommend when children misbehave. So they propose simplistic manipulations of reward and punishment that teach children how to manipulate parents and teachers.

Did you know that none of Freud's theories has ever been conclusively verified? As one of his colleagues accurately said, Freud had a fantastic imagination and a huge ego. Freud believed that if he thought of something, it must be true. Furthermore, he believed he had a responsibility to share his amazing thoughts with the rest of humankind. One of those thoughts was that parenting produces the person. In other words, if an adult has personal problems, it's a sure bet he was parented badly. Even today, most therapists will try to connect a person's problems with aspects of his or her childhood as if there's a clear cause-and-effect relationship. However, it turns out that parenting does not produce the child. It is an influence, and a fairly strong one at that, but lots of very well-adjusted people were parented very badly, and lots of sociopaths were parented very well. In fact, not one of Freud's theories has passed the test of the scientific method. Nevertheless, there are still a good number of therapists who base their treatments on Freud's theories. They aren't threatened with having their licenses taken away. They are more likely to be regarded by their colleagues as having great intellects. Can you imagine a physician treating someone for cancer based on disproven theories from nearly one hundred years ago? It wouldn't happen.

So, yes, I have lost faith in my profession. But please don't conflate my feelings about psychology with a general opinion of psychologists and therapists. I think there are plenty of psychologists and therapists who are helping people more than some of the time. But I am also convinced that providing people with helpful counsel concerning problems of living has nothing to do with how many years one spent in school or the number of impressive degrees one collected during that time. The ability to counsel competently comes from the heart, not the head. Unfortunately, college feeds the head, not the heart. It's as simple as that. When I need advice concerning a problem in my life, I go to a friend who never went to college, but he's got one of the biggest hearts of anyone I've ever known. That's enough qualification for me.

As I have lost faith in my profession, I have become convinced that psychology has been more harmful than helpful where American parenting is concerned. The harm began in the late 1960s, when American parents began taking their marching orders from psychologists and other mental health professionals. Before that time, parents sought advice from elders in their extended families, churches, or communities. The elders in question might not have had more than eight years of formal education, if that, but they were respected for their wisdom about children, and everyone knew that such wisdom could not be acquired in school anyway. These elders gave advice that was common sense as opposed to intellectual. It was based on lives they had led rather than on books they had read. Best of all, their advice cost nothing, and most of the time it worked! I happen to believe that your great-grandmother gave better advice than the average mental health professional of today. The numbers, which I will share in chapter one, tell the story.

America began veering off a well-worn parenting path in the 1960s. During that very tumultuous decade, radical social progressives advocated sweeping changes in every aspect of American society. The old ways were demonized as being not just outmoded but bad, unjust, immoral, and harmful. In some cases—America's general treatment of its nonwhite citizens, for example—that was certainly true. But a few grains of truth were used to make the case for a complete overhaul of society that resulted in the baby being tossed out along with the bathwater. The social reformers promised that if everyone would only climb onto their progressive child-rearing bandwagon, all of America's ills—racism, crime, poverty, gender inequities, mental illness—could be solved.

Of course, the new regime promoted a complete reorganizing and restructuring of society, from the ground up. That fundamental premise drove the demonization of all forms of traditional authority—in government, business, the church, education, corporations, and the military. And it also undermined the authority of parents in the home. Psychologists such as Thomas Gordon, author of the best-selling parenting book of the 1970s, *Parent Effectiveness Training,* said that the traditional exercise of parental authority was the root cause of all child and adult mental health problems. In fact, Gordon said that the traditional practice of parental authority was the root cause of *all* social problems, including poverty, war, and racism. This doctrine was a prime example of the utopianism that defined the era. In effect, Gordon proposed that man and society could be perfected if children were raised according to his immaculate formula. Humility was not one of Gordon's attributes.

The old parenting plan, one that parents had used for hundreds of years, emphasized that parents should raise children who would become responsible members of society. The new plan emphasized the responsibility of parents to ensure their children's happiness and material success. The centerpiece of this new parenting ethos was a new term: high self-esteem. Suddenly, the child and his or her supposed emotional needs became the be-all and end-all of the parenting process.

Just as suddenly, things began going downhill for parents, children, families, schools, communities, and culture. The way children are raised defines what a culture will look like in thirty or so years. Do you think American culture is on the skids? Do you think America was a more civil, polite place fifty years ago than it is today? I do, on both counts. (If you weren't around way back then, I encourage you to find a Bob Hope comedy skit on YouTube.com and compare it to a typical obscenity-laced "comedy" skit from today. Or, compare the lyrics of a song from Smokey Robinson and the Miracles to a popular rap song.) But I also believe we can pull ourselves back from the precipice. To do so, we have to make fundamental changes in how we think about children and how we raise them. That's where culture begins. That's why I wrote this book. I intend to expose the disease and the people who infected us with it, and then I intend to propose not-so-radical solutions. I hope to persuade you to sign on to the retro-revolution.

The Cost
of New Ideas

"There is nothing new under the sun."

—ECCLESIASTES 1:9

A few years ago, I reconnected with a fellow with whom I'd gone to grade school and high school in a Chicago suburb. We shared memories, bringing each other up to date on the trajectories of our lives since we'd walked those not-so-hallowed halls together. In the course of our conversation, he expressed interest in my work. I told him that, through my syndicated newspaper column, books, and public presentations, I promote a return to the parenting philosophy that prevailed before the psychological parenting revolution that took America by storm in the late 1960s and early 1970s and that has had parents by the throat ever since.

"So you believe today's parents should raise kids the way we were raised?" he asked, his skepticism obvious.

"Pretty much," I said. "After all, the outcome was a whole lot better."

"It was?" he asked, incredulous. After all, he and I are both members of a generation led to believe that pre-1960s parenting was benighted (i.e., not guided by all-knowing "experts"). We boomers were also encouraged to construct soap operas out of our childhoods. In these personal dramas, which some members of our generation still let run and ruin their lives, our parents were villains and we were the victims of, at best, their ignorance and, at worst, their emotional and physical (spankings!) abuse.

He was listening, but I could tell by the expression on his face that he didn't quite buy what I was saying. So I took another tack.

I reminded him that the early-1960s population of Proviso West High School in Hillside, Illinois, was just shy of five thousand. I asked him whether he knew of anyone who committed suicide during the four years we were there together. No, he did not, and neither did I. Did he know of anyone who had to be removed from school and placed in a treatment center for alcohol abuse, drug abuse, or incapacitating emotional problems? No, he did not, and neither did I. Any girls who starved themselves to the point of severe emaciation? Nope. Me neither. Anyone who mutilated themselves with razor blades or sharp knives, stuck pins through their eyelids and tongues, or went around dressed in black complaining about how awful life was? No, none of that. How about anyone who physically threatened a teacher or called a teacher a vile name in front of the class? Again, no and no.

I then pointed out to him that every single young person in every high school in America today knows at least one other young person in every one of those categories. That's how much the psychosocial health of America's kids has declined in the past forty years. There is no historical evidence that a crisis of this magnitude in child mental health has ever previously occurred—in *any* culture, much less in America. The irony is that since 1970, American parents have been taking their marching orders from mental health "experts" rather than family and community elders. Correlation does not prove cause, but this particular correlation strongly suggests that professional advice has not advanced the well-being of America's kids. Quite the contrary, it suggests that the purveyors of this high-fallutin' advice have caused a lot more problems than they have solved or ever will solve.

Statistics verify that today's kids are not as happy as kids were in the 1950s and before when, ironically, children were held to higher levels of expectation and responsibility both at home and at school. Examples:

- Nearly every child in the 1950s and before was expected to participate in keeping the house and yard clean and tidy on a daily, unpaid basis. Typically, a child came home from school, changed clothes, performed a routine of chores that took anywhere from thirty minutes to an hour, and then went back outside to play with friends who had performed the same sort of unpaid labor. Furthermore, if a chore was not done properly or completely, the child was called back and told to do it again, after which he was probably sent to his room for the remainder of the day to contemplate the error of his ways. Today's kids, by and large, have no chores. Instead, they have adult-micromanaged after-school and weekend activities that keep them "busy" and "out of trouble" but nowhere near as active as a child of the 1950s. Mind you, the adults in question are very well-intentioned; nonetheless, this micromanagement is misguided. With a nod to the occasional exception, the activities in question are completely irrelevant to anything these kids will be doing as adults. Chores, on the other hand, prepare a child for responsible adulthood. They reduce the chance that a child will ever develop a culturally and personally corrosive entitlement mentality. They prepare a child for responsible, service-oriented citizenship.

◆ The child of the 1950s was held to high standards of behavior. Proper social decorum was taught from the beginning. Before I went to first grade, for example, my mother had taught me to stand aside and let people out of an elevator before I entered. Taking that one example, I travel a lot and spend lots of time in hotels where elevators are the vertical transportation of choice. I can tell you that today's parents, by and large, are not doing a good job of teaching this fundamental courtesy (or most others, for that matter). My mother would have been appalled, and she would have let me know it and probably made me apologize, if I had walked in front of someone without saying "Excuse me," failed to pick up something that someone else had dropped, or failed to look at a person who was talking to me. These are all discourtesies I routinely observe in today's kids of every socioeconomic level and age, and if their parents happen to witness these infractions, they rarely do anything.

◆ If a child in the 1950s misbehaved in school, he was punished at school and he was punished again when he arrived home. It was a formula. And the child's parents did not care to hear the child's side of the story (also known as a lie). Today's typical child operates under some sort of bizarre parent protection program. If a teacher reprimands him at school, he goes home and complains to his parents, who call the school and reprimand the teacher. Nothing of the sort would have occurred in the 1950s. I *never* wanted my parents to find out I'd gotten into trouble elsewhere. Second, if I'd gone home and told my mother that a teacher didn't like me or was picking on me, my mother would have contacted the teacher for the sole purpose of discovering what I was doing to incur her displeasure. Today's child tells his mother that a teacher doesn't like him, and she calls the principal to ask that her child be moved to a different classroom overseen by a more understanding and sensitive teacher. After all, the offending teacher has put her child's self-esteem at risk. If he is not transferred, he may begin to feel bad about himself. Heaven forbid that a child should feel bad about doing bad things. Even if he is a classroom behavior problem, his parents believe his misbehavior is merely a response to bad vibes the teacher is sending in his direction. He is acting out her disapproval, or something along those lines.

◆ Continuing on the subject of school, the child of the 1950s could actually fail tests, fail a subject, and be held back a grade or flunked while his classmates moved on. Furthermore, even if he was an A student and in no danger of failing a grade, his parents and teachers expected him to do his best always. If a C student made a C on a big test, and an A student in the same class also made a C, the A student spent a week or two watching from his bedroom window as the C student played outside. Every time one of today's parents tells me her child has "test anxiety," I have to stifle a big, rude groan. I spent my first through twelfth grades in a state of almost perpetual test anxiety, grade anxiety, flunking anxiety, parent anxiety, teacher anxiety, and principal anxiety. That anxiety contributed greatly to my getting generally good grades and, eventually, a graduate degree. Today's kids need *more* anxiety, not less. After all, if one of them fails a test, he's allowed to take it again. If he has "pervasive undifferentiated test anxiety of unknown origin," he's allowed to take the test on Saturday morning in an empty classroom where one of Beethoven's more soothing concertos is playing, and he can take as much time as he likes. If his parents are dissatisfied with a grade he makes on a test or in a class, the teacher is pressured to change the grade. If she won't, then the parents put pressure on the principal to put pressure on the teacher, and the grade is ultimately changed (because most of today's principals have pervasive undifferentiated parent-phobia). Instead of flunking grades, today's kids are put on what are called "individualized educational plans," where they enjoy the lifelong benefits of lower expectations. By the way, I know these descriptions do not describe *all* of today's parents, but they certainly describe all too many. Not one teacher, principal, or private school headmaster or headmistress I've spoken to in the last twenty years has described today's parents in generally positive terms. They point to exceptions, but they always spend more time talking about the rule.

◆ When the child of the 1950s was punished, it was usually memorable. (Time out had not yet been invented.) Most parents spanked back then, but that generally happened only on "special" occasions. I have asked hundreds of people in my generation, "What is your estimate of the number of spankings you received during your entire childhood?" The average answer is five. We knew that spanking was an option, but the average boomer was not spanked every time he stepped out of line. Nonetheless, the punishments we experienced were not the sort recommended by today's parenting experts. When was the last time you heard of a child being grounded for an entire grading period in a room that was devoid of electronic stimulation? That happened to me in the seventh grade because

I was disruptive in class. How about being grounded for the entire summer between high school graduation and going off to college? That also happened to me. Along with eight other feisty teenage males, I'd been arrested for disturbing the public peace. The charges were eventually dropped, but I was guilty as charged. Neither of those restrictions of my right to run wild shock people my age.

Despite the occasional rigors of growing up in the 1950s, we boomers were a much happier, sturdier, more self-motivated group of kids. Here are some fascinating, if troubling, facts:

◆ According to the best available statistics, today's child is five to ten times more likely than was a child who grew up in the 1950s and 1960s to experience a serious emotional setback by age sixteen.

◆ Since the 1950s, it is estimated that the suicide rate for American children and teens has increased by a factor of ten per capita. In one ten-year period from 1997 to 2007, adolescent suicides increased between 300 and 400 percent.

◆ In the early to mid-1950s, when the adult–child ratio in elementary classrooms was 1 to more than 30 (it is around 1 to 12 today), academic achievement was higher at every grade than it is today, and classroom discipline was not a major issue. It is significant to note that most boomers came to first grade not knowing their ABCs. Yet, sitting in what today would be regarded as criminally overcrowded classrooms, we finished first grade reading at a much higher level, on average, than today's kids. Furthermore, unlike today's parents, ours did not help us with our homework. Our homework was just that: *ours*. It was not our *parents'* homework. And yet, amazingly, we did far better in school, at every grade.

◆ Today's kids are being diagnosed with every disorder under the sun, from ADHD to emotional regulation disorder (the latest from the American Psychiatric Association). No one was diagnosed back then. We were just kids. And lest anyone think we had the same problems but didn't get diagnosed because schools back then didn't work with altruistic mental health professionals who were on the lookout for these disorders, let me set the record straight. It was the rare, very rare, kid who had problems of the sort I'm referring to. There were no mental health professionals employed by or consulting with schools because there weren't enough problems to justify their existence. Women who were teachers in the 1950s have consistently told me they didn't see the kind or number of problems then that they began seeing after 1970. Quite simply, they could not have taught classrooms of thirty-five first graders by themselves, and those thirty-five first graders could not have done so well academically, if the problems in question were in significant existence.

I submit that the primary cause of the drastic deterioration in childhood mental health has taken place because the overwhelming majority of post-1960s mental health professionals have encouraged irrational thinking and, by extension, irrational behavior. They have emphasized the validity of feelings over objectivity, emotions over reasoning, acting out over restraint, and the impulses of passion over the tempering of calm deliberation.

Beginning in the 1960s, mental health professionals encouraged parents to allow their children free emotional expression. They told parents it was better to help their children "get in touch with their feelings" than it was to help them think straight. By the 1970s, public schools had adopted a therapeutic agenda that promoted high self-esteem based on the now disproven idea that the child who felt good about himself would do his best academically. For children, the consequences of this feelings-based upbringing and education include heightened impulsivity, tantrums and other toddler behaviors that last well beyond toddlerhood, and a proclivity toward self-drama that lasts well past adolescence.

I was in graduate school when this trend began. My professors, the authors of the books I read, guest lecturers, and various media talking heads were all saying the same thing: Parents who raised children before the "age of psychological enlightenment" that began in the late 1960s had not allowed their children to express their feelings freely (true, in fact, because people who freely express their feelings are socially obnoxious), and tyrannical parenting had left those kids bereft of full emotional repertoires. Our "inner children" were crying out to be released from bondage and become fully human. The litmus test of fully realized humanity was the ability to express oneself without regard for rigidly repressive (i.e., traditional) social norms. Mental health professionals encouraged people to get in touch with their feelings and "let it all hang out." New therapeutic approaches were constructed around these mantras—gestalt therapy and primal scream therapy, for example. Feelings were suddenly in, and rational deliberation was out. As psychiatrist and best-selling author David Viscott put it:

In feelings there is wisdom, for the simplest feelings speak the greatest truth. . . . Become comfortable with your feelings, because your feelings are your life. . . . Trust your feelings. They're the only true guidance you'll ever get.

This author is only encouraging people to do what many mental health professionals encourage: to get in touch with their feelings and trust them more than they trust their thoughts. The unfortunate fact is that when emotions are not held in check by rational thought, antisocial, irrational, and/or self-destructive behavior is the result.

As we will see, this emphasis on the validity of the irrational infected American parenting in profound ways. The end result is a nation of children at risk.

Two Very Destructive "P" Words

The two most tumultuous decades in the history of the United States were the 1860s and the 1960s. Both were marked by the assassination of a president and a civil war. In the latter case, however, the civil war was one fought not with guns but with competing ideas. Some of the rebels of the 1960s sought to bring about cultural changes that were much needed and long overdue—Martin Luther King and the civil rights movement being the prime example. But King and others like him were cultural renovators. They believed in America's foundational principles and values and sought only to improve the institutions and processes that had been built upon them. But other 1960s rebels were akin to wrecking balls. They set out to destroy our very foundations and then, starting from scratch, build a utopia in which none of the old institutions, including the family, were recognizable. Ultimately, the utopians prevailed, and America was transformed from a nation rooted in tradition and largely informed by the past to one that embraced a postmodern, progressive worldview. Postmodernism was a reaction to the value placed on objectivity by Enlightenment philosophers and scientists such as Newton and Kepler. According to Wikipedia:

Postmodernism postulates that many, if not all, apparent realities are only social constructs and are therefore subject to change. It emphasizes the role of language, power relations, and motivations in the formation of ideas and beliefs. . . . It holds realities to be plural and relative and to be dependent on who the interested parties are and of what their interests consist. It supports the belief that there is no absolute truth and that the way in which different people perceive the world is subjective.

Postmodernism's defining characteristic is the belief that truth is a relative, capricious concept. According to postmodern philosophy, a person's beliefs are merely a function of his or her upbringing, gender, skin color, nationality, socioeconomic status, and the time in history in which he lives. Therefore, truth is not objective; it is a personal or cultural construct, and any current definition of truth is fleeting. Postmodernism rejects the notion that right and wrong are immutable. For the purposes of our discussion, it follows that there is no right way to construct a family or raise children.

Progressivism is the cultural reform movement that arose as the postmodern worldview took hold in the 1960s. Traditionalists (cultural conservatives) believe there is nothing new under the sun; progressives believe in the evolution of ideas and that new ideas are generally better than old ones. The reformers of the 1960s were convinced that society could be perfected if the old ideas and the institutions that perpetuated them were destroyed and radically new ideas and institutions took their places. In effect, they were activists for an American utopia in which there would be no war, racism, poverty, sexism, or even personal problems. The theme song of postmodern utopia was John Lennon's "Imagine," in which he encouraged people to imagine no heaven, hell, countries, religion, greed, or hunger—everyone living in peace and harmony in one "brotherhood of man, sharing all the world." It's a catchy song, but keep in mind that Lennon took lots of mind-altering drugs.

Supposedly, the beliefs and biases that gave rise to and perpetuated the problems targeted by the reformers were instilled during childhood. Therefore, and most important, the family had to be reformed as well, the result being children would hold new, enlightened ideas about humankind.

Most of the progressive family reformers who emerged in the late 1960s were mental health professionals—psychiatrists, psychologists, marriage and family therapists, and family counselors—but some were pediatricians such as T. Berry Brazelton. To attain expert status, all one needed were capital letters after one's name and successful publication of a book or academic paper putting forth revolutionary ideas about marriage and child rearing. The more radical the notion, the better chance it had of getting published.

More than forty years later, it's apparent to anyone who believes in objective facts that the reformers have failed—miserably. America's divorce rate is ten times what it was in the 1950s. More than half of today's kids will spend a significant portion of their childhoods in single-parent homes. As the family breaks down, so does parenting. Child protective service agencies only have enough people-power to deal with the tip of the ever-growing child abuse and neglect iceberg. In 1970, child and family therapists in private practice didn't exist outside large cities, and even then only in wealthy areas. Today, there are more than ten child and family therapists in private practice in my hometown of sixty-five thousand.

How is it that there are more mental health resources than ever, but the mental health of America's kids keeps going downhill? After all, as the number of pediatricians per child has increased, children have become measurably healthier. Why can't the same be said for child and family therapists? The answer, quite frankly, is that pediatricians know what they are doing. Their practices are not based on unverified medical fads; rather, they treat children on the basis of factual information gleaned from scientific research. Many mental health professionals treat patients on the basis of whatever clinical theory is currently in vogue. For example, in the early 1980s, biofeedback therapy was all the rage for treating a broad range of problems, including pervasive anxiety. Few psychologists use biofeedback today. Instead, they use some other therapy that will not be around in thirty years. And lest you think that these new therapies represent advances, let me remind you that no new therapy has slowed the decline in child and adult mental health. So it doesn't matter how many mental health professionals are practicing; child mental health in America will continue to get worse. In fact, the thesis of this book is that it's getting worse in large part *because* of mental health professionals.

The mental health of America's kids is a national scandal. How is it that the country with the most resources has so many kids who wouldn't score five on a mental health scale of one to ten? The answer is that we are paying the price that utopia always demands.

The toll on parents and teachers certainly has been equally profound. Child rearing—something women before the 1960s managed to do fairly casually and matter-of-factly—has become the single most stressful thing a woman will ever do in her adult life. I speak to almost two hundred groups a year, and I frequently ask my audiences to participate in the following two-question survey.

First, I ask, "Does any woman in this audience disagree with the following statement: 'Raising one child today is more stressful to a woman than running a major corporation'?"

I've been asking that question for at least five years—roughly one thousand audiences, large and small. Not once has a woman ever raised a hand in disagreement.

Then I ask, "Does any woman in this audience disagree with this statement: 'Parenting has become bad for the mental health of women'?"

Again, never has a woman raised a hand.

Even men tell me that raising children is the hardest thing they've ever done. I point out that their granddaddies never said or even thought that about raising kids, and I ask, "Why do you think something your grandfather and grandmother thought was fairly straightforward and uncomplicated is the hardest thing you've ever done?"

The typical answer: "Well, John, I mean, um, times have changed, I guess."

Nope, that's not it. Times have *always* changed. Since the *Mayflower* off-loaded in 1620, every generation has brought innovation into American culture. It's called progress, and progress has always been a feature of the American landscape. Furthermore, there have been thirty-year periods in our past during which change was more profound than it has been in the last thirty years, yet child rearing did not change. My grandparents were born around 1890. Times changed more between 1890 and 1920 than they have in the last thirty years. During that time, my grandparents saw the invention of cars, airplanes, the telephone, radio, the first global war, and the birth of the first communist state. My parents were born around 1920, and again, more change occurred from 1920 to 1950 than has occurred in the last thirty years. Think of the changes brought about by the Great Depression, World War II, the invention of the atomic bomb, jet airplanes, and television! But in both of those historical periods, with everything imaginable changing, the way people raised children did not change. In fact, people realized that in times of change, certain things must remain constant to prevent change from producing chaos, and one of those things was how children were raised.

No, the explanation for why parenting has become so difficult for all concerned in the first forty years of the postmodern era is not that times have changed. The explanation is that America's foundational principles were attacked, and the revolutionaries tossed the baby out with the bathwater. We became persuaded that everything under the sun had to change, and we are now paying the price.

It's not much different for teachers. I talk to hundreds of them, individually and in groups, on a yearly basis. Many of those who have been teaching for twenty years or more tell me they no longer enjoy what they do, at least not nearly as much as they did when they started. Many are continuing to teach only because they have too much invested in their retirement accounts to stop now. Over the past twenty years, they've seen the behavior of children deteriorate, learning problems proliferate, and cooperation with parents evaporate.

I am a member of the last generation of American children to be raised the old, traditional way, and I am a member of the first generation of American parents to begin raising children the new way. I was just entering graduate school when my wife and I had our first child. My graduate school professors were excited about the new way of raising children—or *parenting,* as it was coming to be known—so the new way is what they taught, and that's what I learned. I took these new ideas home and persuaded my wife, who was the second of seven children and had grown up in a very traditional family, to help me implement them. And we learned the hard way, at a painful personal level, that they didn't work. Furthermore, it doesn't matter how hard one works at them. The new parenting ideas don't work, period. They are dysfunctional, and no amount of effort will make them functional.

The Nitty-Gritty

It's now time to get down to specifics and answer the question, "What are the differences between traditional (pre-1970) child rearing and what I call postmodern psychological parenting?" In the following section, I may sound as if I'm criticizing today's parents, but I am critiquing, not criticizing, and there's a vast difference. I'm trying to help parents understand what psychological parenting propaganda has done to them, how it has turned them into their own worst enemies, how the new parenting they practice is not bringing out the best in their children. Then, as the book unfolds, I'm going to spell out an uncomplicated program for recovery. But first, let's explore the differences.

From Honoring to Dishonoring

To begin, the most obvious difference is that parents of the traditional era honored their mothers and fathers by staying true to form when raising their own children. They took the parenting baton from their parents, carried it with reverence, and when it was time, they passed it on to their young adult children. By contrast, postmodern parenting is informed by the opinions of so-called parenting experts. And remember, I am considered to be one of them. Therefore, I see the problem from the inside. I was trained as a disciple of New Parenting, and I carried its banner for a while. I lived it in my family, and I recovered from its toxicity. I'm like the guy who leads a twelve-step group: been there, done that.

The advice given by "parenting experts" is nothing like the advice a pre-1960 mom received from her mother. For one thing, her mother didn't charge and didn't give expensive batteries of tests to create the illusion that something scientific was being done to arrive at a diagnosis, which she didn't deal in either. Great-Grandma dispensed common sense that came from the accumulated child-rearing wisdom of many generations. The new expert class dispenses theory, speculation, and therapies whose validity has not been proven. Why, the experts don't even agree among themselves! Nonetheless, they all manage to get published. That's the essence of postmodernity; there is no one right way. All expert opinions are equal, even when they stand in opposition to one another. The only certainty is that the old way is, well, old, and no longer relevant.

Did you know that as of May 2012, Amazon.com listed sixty-eight thousand parenting books? Imagine them placed one atop the other. I call the resulting mile-high stack of books the "Tower of Parent-Babble," hence the title of this book. Like the story in the Old Testament Book of Genesis, chapter eleven, this postmodern tower of blah-blah-blah has caused nothing but confusion.

From What? to Why?

Since the 1960s, the focus has shifted away from what children actually do, especially when the doing involves misbehavior, to the question of why they do it. The postmodern parenting paradigm emphasizes the primacy of a child's feelings. As my graduate school child psychology professor repeatedly emphasized, a child's misbehavior is merely a way of calling attention to an underlying conflicted feeling state. Don't get distracted by the behavior, he would say; figure out what lies hidden beneath. This also represents a shift from the objective to the subjective, from the verifiable to the speculative, from the rational to the irrational. Disagreement about what is in the best interests of children is the inevitable result.

Two psychologists can agree that ten-year-old Billy threw a rock through a neighbor's window with deliberate aim. But no two psychologists will completely agree about *why* Billy threw the rock in the first place. Come to think of it, the neighbor looks somewhat like the father who abandoned the family six months ago and hasn't been seen since. Is Billy simply trying, in some desperate way, to discharge pent-up anger at a father who deserted him just as he was approaching puberty? Yes, that's it!

That is, by the way, the way my graduate school professors taught me to think. Note that this explanation, like every other psychological explanation of antisocial behavior, magically transforms Billy from a perpetrator into a victim. Had Billy broken the neighbor's window in 1957, that would have been the long and the short of it. He broke the window—end of story, except for whatever punishment his parents decided upon. Furthermore, they would not have listened to any of his clever excuses. It is a given that Billy would have had to figure out how to pay the neighbor for the window, perhaps by mowing and weeding his yard for two years.

But what happens to a rock-throwing, window-breaking Billy today? One thing is certain: He can't be punished. That would be punishing him for having valid feelings. As for the broken window, well, the good news is that we now know Billy is in psychic pain. So, his case is probably discussed by a group of professionals who decide that Billy needs weekly therapy sessions with a mental health professional who will end up giving him the impression that having an absent father is an excuse to act on any outrageous impulse that comes along. This much is perfectly clear: No one is going to hold Billy accountable. That is, in fact, what too many mental health professionals end up doing when they counsel children: They make matters worse rather than better. They send children the message that they have valid reasons for disrespecting and disobeying adults (their parents aren't meeting their psychological needs), being destructive (they're angry at their parents), and so on.

From Leadership to Relationship

The old paradigm emphasized the need for parents to provide firm, loving leadership for children. Through this leadership, effectively and ethically delivered, the child was able to leave childish things (narcissism, self-absorption, jealousy, irresponsibility in various forms, self-drama) behind and eventually become a responsible adult citizen in possession of compassion, respect for others, and a solid work ethic.

The new paradigm emphasizes the need for parents to be in close *relationship* with their children. The problem is that when a person in a leadership position attempts to establish a close relationship with the people he is leading, his effectiveness as a leader is canceled. Children need leadership, at least until they have developed good impulse control. Under the best circumstances, that does not occur until age thirteen—one reason behind the Jewish Bar Mitzvah, which celebrates the thirteen-year-old young man's attainment of self-discipline. After the purpose of parent leadership has been fulfilled, *then* relationship can be developed. Putting the cart before the horse, which today's parents are unwittingly doing, doesn't work. The inevitable end result is a child who is still underdisciplined at age thirteen. That explains why so many of today's teens act irrationally so often and why some act irrationally nearly all the time. Believe it or not, the contemporary notion that teens are naturally rebellious, disrespectful, petulant, moody, and self-absorbed is not verified historically, not in the least.

In 1830, Alexis de Toqueville came to America from Europe for the purpose of studying our fledgling democracy. He wrote a two-volume book, *Democracy in America,* based on his observations and experiences. In it, he describes the American adolescent as trustworthy, responsible, hardworking, a good neighbor. Toqueville had not one negative thing to say about American teenagers, but today's teens are quite a different story. Remember, it's not because *times* have changed, nor have children changed. In this case, it's because today's parents do not provide proper leadership during years three to thirteen, when a child's need for leadership is paramount.

The notion that relationship is the centerpiece of good parenting is completely embedded in the American mindset. Whenever I assert that *leadership* is the primary parental function during what I call the decade of discipline (three to thirteen), and relationship needs to take the backseat, people become confused. Some even become angry. Many parents interpret this to mean that I'm telling them not to express affection to their children or have fun with them. They also seem to think that if they don't put relationship first, their kids will not feel free to come to them with problems. I am not saying anything of the sort. I am simply pointing out that relationship has almost completely displaced leadership in American parenting, and this deprives children of what they need from parents in order to develop proper impulse control and think of others first instead of themselves.

This is not incompatible with showing affection or having fun. If proper leadership is provided, disciplinary problems are held to a minimum and interactions between parents and children are much more relaxed and affectionate. Communication between parents and child will improve because the child will regard his parents with respect; he will come to them more often for advice. And because of the relaxation that pervades the family, everyone will have a much better time with one another.

From Love and Leadership to Love Alone

The old paradigm emphasized a balance of love and discipline. The new paradigm puts the child's need for love above his need for discipline. The problem is that when love leaves its moorings, it becomes purely emotional. The inevitable result is drama and enabling. In this regard, the number one complaint I hear from principals, heads of schools, veteran teachers, and school counselors is that all too many of today's parents are world-class enablers. Simply put, they do for their children what their children are capable of doing for themselves and cannot accept that their children do wrong things. They do their children's homework, for example. Mind you, these parents would say they are only helping, but the end result is homework without error. Clearly, that result is not obtained unless parents are doing more than a little legitimate consulting here and there.

When their children misbehave at school, instead of supporting teachers, they become their kids' advocates and attorneys. They make excuses for them and even point the finger of blame at the teacher who reported the problem. They accuse the teacher, who may be a forty-something professional who has dedicated her life to the betterment of the lives of children, of having it in for the child, or something equally absurd. Many of today's parents seem to believe that truly loving parents do all they can to make sure their children never experience pain, failure, frustration, or disappointment. Unfortunately, in real life, enabling *always* weakens the person being enabled. That goes a long way toward explaining the sharp increase in the average age of male emancipation since 1970, when it was between twenty and twenty-one.

From Citizenship to Self-ship

The pre-1960 parent's purpose was to raise a good citizen, a person of character who would have and show respect for others, be a good neighbor, possess a solid work ethic, be compassionate and charitable to those less fortunate, be willing to set aside self-interest to serve community and country, take on necessary responsibilities, accept personal accountability, and obey the law. (It is significant to note that Toqueville described the typical 1830s American adolescent in much the same way.) By contrast, today's parents are focused on their children's esteem for themselves and their supposed *needs*, by which they do not mean the absolute necessities of air, food, water, and protection from the elements and wild animals. Rather, they are referring to entitlements such as the "right" teacher, adjustments to the school curriculum that are in line with the child's learning style, adequate praise and reward for doing what is expected, and being treated "fairly" (being protected from failure and disappointment).

Today's parents, by and large, suffer from tunnel vision, and the entire visual field at the end of any parent's tunnel is his or her child. Actually, children also suffer from their parents' tunnel vision. They don't learn how to solve their own problems. They don't develop adequate coping skills when it comes to failure, disappointment, and the inevitable unfairness of reality. That explains why today's kids are so vulnerable to depression and other incapacitating emotional problems: They have been so protected from reality that when they run head-on into it, they collapse instead of picking themselves up, dusting themselves off, and pressing on with increased resolve. The practice of giving every child on the team the same trophy, as if no one's play stands out from anyone else's, is certainly well intentioned, but we have all heard about the road so paved.

Pre-1960 parents were trying to raise children who as adults would make contributions that strengthened America and made it a better place. Their purpose was *large*. It was about their children's future citizenship. Today's parents are trying to raise children who "feel good about themselves" (have high self-esteem) and believe the fantasy that they are capable of doing whatever they want to do as adults. That parenting purpose is small, individualistic, and unrealistic. It does harm to the child, and it does harm to America.

From Macromanagement to Micromanagement

As relationship displaced leadership and concern for the self displaced the goals of good citizenship and neighborliness, parents became involved—in everything. Today's parents keep social calendars for their children from age two on so they can keep track of "play dates." They arrange their children's after-school and weekend activities. They help their children with their homework. They pick out the clothes their kids wear to church and school. They oversee almost every waking moment of their children's lives, making sure every detail is just so.

My generation grew up during a time when adults left children pretty much to their own devices. They were there for us in the event of a crisis, but even then they often did not define crisis the way we defined it. Pre-1960 parents expected their children to solve their own social problems, entertain and occupy themselves, do their chores without reminders, do their own homework, organize their own games, wash their own cuts, put on their own bandages, and get their own snacks. As a consequence, children learned by trial and error to be responsible for themselves. Let's face it: In the final analysis, the feeling that "I'm competent" will take a person a lot further than the feeling that "I'm special."

Another way of saying this is that the pre-1960s child learned how to *keep* his parents from getting involved. The unspoken but clear message from parent to child was, "Respect and obey adults in positions of legitimate authority, do your schoolwork to the best of your ability, treat other children with respect, play fair, obey the rules, do your chores without being reminded, and I will leave you alone." That was certainly my parents' message to me. When I stepped out of line, broke a rule, acted irresponsibly, *then* they got involved, and not always in ways I desired, believe me. I quickly learned to keep them from having to manage me by simply managing myself in a responsible fashion. My childhood experience in the 1950s and early 1960s was very typical. When I describe my upbringing to people older than fifty-five, they always say that was how they were brought up as well.

It's clear to anyone my approximate age and older that micromanagement is the norm in parenting today. Furthermore, this widespread micromanagement is generally regarded as the parenting ideal. It's what today's parents think is not only right and proper but absolutely necessary. That's too bad, because micromanagement *always* creates a set of predictable problems: conflict, irresponsibility, codependency, deceit, and disloyalty.

Those consequences summarize the problems today's parents most often complain to me about:

◆ They have conflict with their kids in the form of frequent arguments that often end with screaming and seething anger and then guilt.

◆ Their kids act irresponsibly when it comes to such things as schoolwork, even small household requests, getting ready for school or church in the morning, picking up after themselves, and keeping their rooms neat and clean.

◆ Their kids say "I can't" a lot, wanting the parents to solve their problems, even small problems such as being hungry in the middle of the day.

◆ Their kids hide stuff from them and lie about even insignificant things.

- ◆ When they become teens and can finally get out from under the oppressive micromanagement that's been going on for thirteen years, the kids rebel and begin acting in ways that are completely contrary to their parents' values.

- ◆ The kids go off to college, can't cope with the requirements of independent living, collapse, and come back home in the form of dependent adult children if not basket cases. In other words, the pigeons come home to roost.

From Boundaries to Virtually None

Along with the emphasis on relationship and involvement, the long-standing boundary between the culture of adults and the culture of children has dissolved. Once upon a time not so long ago, children had reason to look up to adults. Adults lived in a different world, breathed a different atmosphere, spoke a different language, and laughed at things they wouldn't explain to children. They even sat at a different table at family gatherings, talking and laughing about adult mysteries. Adults wrapped themselves in mystique. Therefore, children *wanted* to become adults because that was the only way the mysteries would reveal themselves. They *wanted* to grow up.

Do today's young people really want to grow up? It often doesn't look like it. The toddler-esque clothes that many young men wear—baggy shorts, oversized T-shirts, sneakers, flat-billed baseball caps worn backwards—certainly do not suggest a desire to be responsible citizens. Young adults are often found still living at home, freeloading off their parents until their late twenties—some even later. Many of them are adamant about not wanting to ever get married and have children. When they finally emancipate, many of them live beyond their means and end up coming back home to freeload some more.

Experts have convinced many of today's parents that a lack of boundaries is characteristic of good parenting. The tip of this iceberg is the new practice of children and parents sleeping in the same "family bed." This practice is promoted by certain experts as essential to proper "bonding," but there is a complete lack of compelling evidence to that effect. This is babble, pure and simple, and I discuss it later in this book.

In many other ways, postmodern parenting experts encourage the mother to be at her children's constant beck and call. They address this to *mothers,* mind you. As a consequence, today's mother often feels that her kids are constantly intruding on her privacy and purpose. They interrupt her as soon as she gets on the phone, as soon as she engages in conversation with someone in public, as soon as she begins doing anything for herself. Many moms have even told me their kids often walk in on them when they're on the toilet or taking a shower. The problem in these instances is not the children. The problem is that the mother in question does not feel she has the right to tell her children what the pre-1960 mom often said to her kids: "You're bothering me. Leave me alone. Go outside and find something to do, or I'll find something for you to do. And don't come home until dinnertime, or I'll put you to work around here."

A critic of mine once said that sort of talk from mother to child was harsh. I pointed out that when my mom said words to that effect to me, I didn't feel it to be harsh. I wasn't hurt or saddened. I just thought she was having a bad day. I also pointed out that my generation left home earlier than today's kids are leaving home, did better in school, and had much better mental health. If 1950s mothering was harsh, then harsh mothering must be good.

Boundaries are essential to respect. The alternative is being taken for granted. And sure enough, that is what many mothers tell me: They feel their children take them for granted.

The bottom line is that the experts encourage mothers to lower their personal boundaries where their kids are concerned, their children respond by taking advantage and taking them for granted, and mothers end up feeling that raising kids is the most stressful, draining thing they've ever done.

The Toll on Kids

When managing their children's emotional states became more important to parents than teaching them how to think correctly, children became increasingly dramatic and emotional. Why do some teens engage in promiscuous sex? They aren't thinking straight. They're creatures of emotion. Why do some teens cut themselves, wrap themselves in doom and gloom, and commit suicide? They aren't thinking straight. They're creatures of emotion. Why do some children still throw public tantrums when they are eight years old? They aren't thinking straight. They're creatures of emotion. Why do some children consistently underperform in school, oblivious to the consequences? They aren't thinking straight. They're creatures of emotion. In each case, the child is "thinking" with his or her feelings.

Feelings are fine things sometimes. They are a large part of what it means to be a human being. But if feelings are not tamed by straight thinking, they can drive highly impulsive, irrational, even self-destructive behavior. Too many of today's kids are not thinking straight, even as teenagers, whereas young people were once expected to do so and did.

Let me take the reader back to the encounter with my high school friend that opened this chapter. The only explanation for why, in a high school of nearly five thousand students in the early 1960s, my friend and I do not remember anyone who abused drugs or alcohol, committed suicide, cut themselves with razor blades, threatened a teacher, or had to be taken out of school and put in a treatment center is that we were thinking straight, as straight as possible for kids fourteen to nineteen years old. We had emotions, sure, but we were not enslaved to them.

And the only possible explanation for the fact that we teenage boomers had learned to control our emotions reasonably well is that our parents didn't give one ounce of energy to promoting our esteem for ourselves. Instead, they raised us to be good citizens, respect other people, display good manners, help others in need, be good neighbors, do our best, respect their boundaries (and other people's), obey adults in positions of legitimate authority, and make sure they didn't have to get involved in our lives. In short, they taught us to think with our brains, not our feelings.

It wasn't a complicated undertaking then, and it is not a complicated undertaking now.

Authority
Babble

*"Football is like life. It requires perseverance,
self-denial, hard work, sacrifice, dedication,
and respect for authority."*

—VINCE LOMBARDI

Someday, I just might write a book titled *Things Your Great-Grandmother Would* Never *Have Said*. It will be a collection of "parent-isms," silly things parents have said to me over the years, such as, "I'm not rushing into toilet training because I don't want my son to develop issues around retention and elimination." No kidding, a mother actually said that to me once.

Actually, parents say things like that to me fairly often. They do so because they read too much (an ironic thing for me to say). This almost obsessive reading—especially on the part of mothers—has caused them to intellectualize parenting, something that comes naturally from the heart. Parenting does not come naturally from the head. The head is the seat of worry, stress, anxiety, and guilt—the negative feelings that infuse today's child rearing. If good parenting came from the head, then the smartest people would be the best parents, but I haven't noticed that to be the case. Have you?

My great-grandmother book will also include the story of a mom who asked my advice about her two preschool boys, both of whom talked back to her and refused to do what she asked them to do. Turned out she did exactly that—asked—and her boys took understandable advantage of the obvious loophole. She told me she didn't feel comfortable "ordering them around," by which she meant using unequivocal language such as, "I want you to pick up your toys now." In that situation, she would ask whether they might be inclined to perhaps consider giving her a hand with picking up their toys or something equally equivocal. When I asked why she felt uncomfortable with authoritative instructions, she said, "I want them to question authority. Plus, I want to respect their need for self-expression and make them feel like they can always speak freely to me."

"Well," I said, "It's obvious that you've already accomplished those objectives."

Things have really changed now that parenting has turned into a project focused on deep (theoretical) psychological qualities. Parenting used to be about children's values, character, and behavior. The primary parent–child understanding was quite simple: Parents told children what to do, and children did what they were told. Children occasionally tried to get away with misbehavior, but only when they thought adults weren't looking. Outright, face-to-face defiance or disrespect was pretty much unheard of.

It seems that this wasn't a good thing, however. Psychologist Thomas Gordon (1918–2002), the author of *Parent Effectiveness Training,* one of the best-selling parenting books of the 1970s, maintained that the only reason the 1950s child obeyed his parents was fear of what would happen if he did not. That's certainly not consistent with my experience. My mother was a single parent for most of the first seven years of my life. She didn't threaten, yell, spank, or do anything else to induce terror, yet I obeyed her. In fact, I don't remember ever being punished. I'm certain it happened, but it was not a regular ingredient in my childhood. She gave me a stern talking-to from time to time, but even that wasn't the norm. She did not give me rewards for obedience either—she had no time for such nonsense.

Testing Gordon's theory beyond my own experience, I've spoken with lots of people my age and older about their childhoods, asking whether they obeyed their parents. I have yet to meet someone my age who did not. Then I ask, "What methods or techniques did your parents use to make you obedient?"

Most of my peers tell me that their parents didn't use methods. They simply made their expectations perfectly clear. The parents in question weren't perfect, and not every parent back then was equally effective, but the overwhelming majority brought a calm confidence to their responsibilities. They communicated that confidence in the way they spoke to their kids, and their kids responded by doing what they were told. And remember, *all the available evidence says that children raised in the 1950s and before were a whole lot happier, on average, than today's kids.*

Then along came Gordon, who published his paradigm-changing work in 1970, the final year of the most paradigm-changing decade in American history. In the absence of any compelling evidence, he independently decided that the basic principles parents had been following and the ways they'd been doing things for several hundred years in America and thousands of years in the rest of the world were bad for children. The traditional exercise of parental authority, Gordon asserted, caused children to develop gnawing psychological problems that prevented them from becoming fully realized human beings. They grew up emotionally and intellectually stunted but never able to put their fingers on the problem. Gordon decided what the problem was, and then he decided that he was going to lead the rescue operation.

I hold Gordon primarily responsible for the conundrum faced by the young mom in the previous example. She wanted her preschool boys to respect and obey her, but she had read somewhere or heard on some talk show that parents should not "force" their authority on their kids. They should handle parent–child conflict as if they were negotiating with other adults, with mutually acceptable compromise being the goal.

That's Gordon's legacy. As a result of his mischief, many of today's parents are wishy-washy when it comes to setting limits and giving instructions. They don't discipline with purpose. They negotiate with their kids. They want their kids to like them. That's the short list. No one has benefited from what Gordon set in motion, yet he was nominated for the Nobel Peace Prize three times, and both the American Psychological Foundation and the California Psychological Association presented him with lifetime achievement awards. After all, his ideas were *new*.

When Authority Was a Good Thing

Pre-1960s parents understood something very important: *A child needs unwavering authority from his parents as much as he needs their unconditional love.* Pre-1960s mothers and fathers understood that figuring out and meeting their kids' theoretical psychological needs was not part of their job description. It was their responsibility to produce good citizens, people who would make America a better place. Their children's future citizenship was the goal, and molding proper character was the immediate issue. They recognized that authority was a key element in this construction project.

Since the 1960s, the overwhelming majority of modern psychology's parenting prophets have preached that parents should abandon the old ways, including the very notion that they are authority figures. The prophets told parents to treat their children as equals, explain themselves, and resolve disagreements by arriving at compromises. And many American parents did and continue to do exactly that. Why not? After all, people tend to believe that "experts" know what they're talking about. Unfortunately, most of the postmodern parenting gurus have *not* known what they were talking about. They were making it all up. And they were dead wrong.

Since the late 1960s, American parents have been consistently misled by people who believed their opinions were the final word on the subject. That was certainly true of Thomas Gordon. He said the traditional exercise of parent authority was bad, but we now know beyond a reasonable doubt—based on research I will describe that has been carried out by impartial people—that traditional parent authority is much better for kids than the alternative Gordon described. In fact, the research says there is no better alternative. Without question, there are parents who overdiscipline, whose expectations are unreasonable, and who fail to demonstrate adequate love for their children. But to point out that there are parents who do harm is very different from claiming that parental authority, in and of itself, is harmful.

The Stage Is Set; the Star Walks On

In the 1960s, Gordon began teaching a revolutionary new approach to communication between parents and children. In 1970, he published his seminar in book form in *Parent Effectiveness Training* (PET). It quickly became the bible for anyone who worked with parents and children. Family counselors embraced Gordon's model, and it began to spread widely. Several years later, Gordon followed up with *Teacher Effectiveness Training,* in which he applied his methods to the classroom.

In *Parent Effectiveness Training,* Gordon laments that "parents today rely almost universally on the same methods of raising children and dealing with problems in their families that were used by their own parents, by their parents' parents, by their grandparents' parents." That's a prime example of postmodern progressive thinking, with its implicit assumption that new ideas are better than old ideas. Why are they better? Because they are new! Oh, of course. Apparently no one noticed the circular thinking.

Until Gordon came along, it was axiomatic that parents raised their children the way they themselves had been raised. By adopting the parenting model they had learned as children, they "honored their mothers and fathers." That's the fifth of the Ten Commandments, and it is the only one that carries a promise: "and you will live long in the land the Lord God has given you." Indeed, it had long been universally recognized that culture building began with the raising of children. The stability of a culture over time required that its child-rearing traditions be passed down unchanged from generation to generation and that every generation *honor* the previous generation's sincere attempt to do the job properly. In other words, when people begin tinkering with a culture's child-rearing traditions, causing a generation of parents to take off in a completely different direction, they introduce instability into the culture. They weaken it. Ultimately, they threaten its very existence.

But Gordon's parenting propaganda, although lacking in evidence, was exciting. It fit perfectly with the times, which is why he was able to convince parents and professionals alike that raising children the "old" way was akin to treating pneumonia with a steady diet of chicken soup.

Gordon's War on Authority

The core of Gordon's ideology is the notion that relationships based on power and authority—*any authority*—are wrong, immoral, and unjust. He preached that the end result of the traditional parenting model, because it failed to recognize and meet the psychological needs of children, drove them to misbehave or become self-destructive.

> *One of the last sanctions for the use of power in human relationships is in the home—in the parent–child relationship. . . . Why are children the last ones to be protected against the potential evils of power and authority? As more people begin to understand power and authority more completely and accept its use as unethical . . . [parents] will begin to feel that it is just as immoral in those relationships.*

Notice that Gordon isn't saying parents can abuse their authority; he's saying parent authority is potentially evil, unethical, and immoral. He's saying that it can't be used properly; in and of itself, it is toxic.

According to Gordon, even a child who seems content to submit to his or her parents, who appears to be accepting and thriving under a traditional, authoritative family paradigm, really isn't. His compliance is nothing more than a coping mechanism. The child is merely retreating into himself, the long-term effect of which is bound to be a dependent, timid, cowering person who never learns to fend for or stand up for himself.

Some children . . . cope through submission, obedience, and compliance. . . . [They] continue to be submissive and compliant through early adolescence and often into adulthood. . . . These are the adults who remain children throughout their lives, passively submitting to authority, denying their own needs, fearing to be themselves, frightened of conflict, too compliant to stand up for their own convictions. These are adults who fill the offices of psychologists and psychiatrists.

In this passage, Gordon evoked the then-popular notion that an "inner child" resided within the psyche of every adult and that the health of this being, as determined by childhood experience, was synonymous with the psychological health of the "outer" person. Was the inner child happy and content, or was it huddled fearfully in a corner of the subconscious mind, having been denied its psychological rights (autonomy) by tyrannical parents? If the latter, then the individual was certainly in need of some liberating form of therapy, of which ever-stranger varieties—primal scream therapy, for example—were proliferating at the time.

I happen to agree with Gordon about the existence of an inner child. I concluded long ago that lurking inside every one of us is a toddler who still believes that he's the Chosen One, deserving of special consideration, entitled to special privilege, and that everyone should immediately bend to his every whim. The inner toddler is self-absorbed, rude, and selfish; he demands attention and throws tantrums when he doesn't get his way. Even the most well-socialized, responsible person has occasional inner toddler episodes. Keeping him under *complete* control would require constant vigilance and more energy than a person could sustain. But it's possible, even considering the occasional jailbreaks, to keep him *controlled,* and that is every civilized person's task. Whereas Gordon wants to liberate him, I want to keep him in solitary confinement for life.

Family Anarchy

Gordon proposed that parents create democratic families in which parents and children coexist as emotional, social, and intellectual equals. Obviously, Gordon idealized and romanticized children. He went beyond believing they were innately pure; he believed that children were little adults who had a psychological right to be treated as such and even enjoy many adult privileges. To significant extent, his philosophy informed the children's rights movement that was then beginning to gain traction in both America and Europe.

For example, Gordon asserted that "democratic relationships produce greater health and well-being." That's certainly true of adult relationships, but he was arguing that children are better off when adults do not exercise authority in their lives. He advised that any dispute between parent and child should be resolved in a manner that allows the child to retain self-respect and autonomy. Gordon called it "no-lose" conflict resolution. This egalitarian method involved active listening (e.g., "I hear you saying that you're not comfortable with my decision"), negotiation, and compromise of the sort that might occur between a husband and wife when they disagree on whether to take vacation at Disney World or Las Vegas. On any given occasion, the goal is to reach agreement that results in everyone being happy.

One reason Gordon's theories sold well is that it all sounded convincing. The problem was that it didn't work. In the mid-1970s, I attended a PET seminar conducted by one of Gordon's disciples. I had been sent by my bosses at the community mental health center where I was directing an early intervention program for children and families. The intent was that I would learn Gordon's methods, teach them to parents with whom I worked, and make Gastonia, North Carolina, a model of family harmony for the rest of the world to marvel at.

When the instructor (actually, he called himself a "facilitator" because the idea that he was an instructor smacked of, well, authority) began talking about Gordon's "no-lose" conflict resolution, he made the statement that it could be used with children as young as two. At the time, my son was six and my daughter was three. I had a good reality-based sense of what living with a two-year-old was like, so I challenged him. We went back and forth for a while (he was definitely unwilling to compromise on this issue), getting nowhere. Finally, somewhat exasperated, he proposed that we role-play a parent–child conflict in which the child in question was a toddler. I agreed to that. He proposed that he play the parent and I play the toddler. I agreed to that as well. He then proposed that he stand but that I get on my knees so I could experience the interaction from a child's point of view. Fine. I then proposed that the confrontation take place in a store. I, toddler, want Daddy to buy me a fire truck that's caught my eye. He, Daddy, cannot make the purchase because he doesn't have enough money, a credit card, or a check. He agreed to that, and we were off and running.

Holding an imaginary truck, I said, "I want this."

Bending over to get down to my level, so my inner child wouldn't feel intimidated by his outer adult, he said, "That is a really nice fire truck, Johnny! You certainly have an eye for fire trucks! If I was you, I'd want that fire truck too! Unfortunately, Daddy doesn't have the money to buy you the fire truck today. Maybe we can come back some other day and get this fire truck! Okay?"

"No! I want this fire truck now!"

"Johnny, I hear you saying that you want to take that fire truck home with you, but Daddy can't buy the fire truck today, Johnny. See? (He held open an imaginary wallet.) Daddy doesn't have any money, and the man who owns the store wants me to give him money for the fire truck."

Attracting the attention of everyone in this imaginary store, I yelled, "I want this fire truck!"

"Johnny, I hear you saying that the fire truck is really nice, and you want the fire truck. Hey, Johnny, I have an idea! How about if we go home and put up a chart on the refrigerator, and every time you're a big boy and help Mommy and Daddy with something like picking up your toys, I'll put a star on your chart, and when you have five stars we'll come back and get this really nice fire truck!"

Unimpressed by promises of stars on a chart, I opened my mouth and bellowed, "I WANT THIS FIRE TRUCK NOW!" at the top of my toddler lungs. Everyone in the room recoiled at the shock.

The instructor stood up, glared at me, and said (now addressing the adult me, still on my knees), "That's enough! This is pointless! You're refusing to play by any rules!"

The room was suddenly quiet as his last seven words hung in the air. Everyone was sitting stock still, eyes wide open, waiting for my response.

"You're right," I said. "I'm not playing by any rules."

I'm really not sure he got it. Needless to say, I was persona non grata for the rest of the seminar. I received my certification, but only because denying it would have violated one of Gordon's foremost principles: Don't punish a child for misbehaving (I'll get to that in an upcoming chapter).

Gordon's conflict resolution methods work well for adults who are emotionally and intellectually mature and willing to set aside self-interest for the purpose of achieving a creative relationship. That means Gordon's methods won't even work for some adults. If one party in a dispute is, in effect, a child—self-centered and interested only in winning at whatever cost—Gordon's methods are worthless. It takes some time for a child to realize the wisdom of giving up the enticement of short-term gain in favor of long-term reward. I'm not talking only about the ability to postpone gratification; I'm also referring to a person's ability to realize that a lasting relationship is more important than getting what he wants. That does not define a child.

In the 1950s, Gordon had served as a consultant to business organizations. During this time, he developed Leader Effectiveness Training, a program that trained managers and executives in negotiating and conflict resolution skills. Gordon eventually decided the same methods would work in parent–child relationships as well as they did between coworkers or employer and employee, so he built Parent Effectiveness Training on the Leader Effectiveness Training template. Unfortunately, what worked for the geese did not work for the goslings. Even more unfortunate, very few people seemed to understand that it wasn't going to work, and even fewer were willing to admit that it *wasn't* working. The message to parents who tried and failed with Gordon's methods was that the failure meant something was wrong with them rather than a failed paradigm. Maybe they weren't being consistent, or they were control freaks and unwilling to relinquish authority over their kids. Having been the victims of parental authority themselves, their need to "pass it on" by victimizing their own children prevented them from using PET principles properly.

Gordon was unable to see any fault in his reasoning. In the early 1980s, I wrote a newspaper column in which I criticized his opposition to parental authority. By then, my column was appearing in more than one hundred papers nationwide, including a handful in his home state of California. Gordon wrote my syndicate a letter, protesting that I had misrepresented him. He claimed that he *did* believe in parents having authority over their children. Really?

I went to his book, lifted several quotes—some of the same ones used in this chapter—and put them in a follow-up column. I sent the column to him, inviting him to respond. I never heard another word.

The Age of Aquarius

Gordon thought that his family model represented more than just a new approach to household relationships. He saw it as a prototype that could transform humanity and produce a worldwide, violence-free utopia.

Democratic families are peaceful families, and when there are enough democratic families, we will have a society that rejects violence and finds warfare unacceptable.

The implication is that families in which parental authority is the norm are largely to blame for the violence and wars that have occurred throughout history. In a later book, *Teaching Children Self-Discipline,* Gordon speculates that if families and schools were run democratically and children were free of the tyranny of adult authority, the results would include less juvenile delinquency, alcoholism, reckless driving, drug abuse, rape, gang violence, homicide, premarital pregnancies, and hopelessness. Because teachers and students would get along better, student motivation and grades would improve along with truancy and dropout rates. Gordon even says that if the world adopted his parenting methods, fewer wars would result. In short, Gordon actually believed he held the secret to creating a perfect world.

Unfortunately, as the reader will soon see, the best research into parenting outcomes has found that children raised according to Gordon's parenting ideal have *more* adjustment difficulties than children raised by parents who are the very sort of authority figures he rails against. If Gordon's methods don't improve children, they definitely are not going to improve the world.

Gordon urged mothers and fathers to replace authoritative direction, which communicates the expectation of obedience, with "active listening," in which parents respond to a child's statements and protests by repeating them, as in, "I hear you saying you want the fire truck, Johnny." The goal is to communicate respect for the child's feelings. The alleged result will be parents who better understand the true needs of their children and children who feel truly respected by their parents. According to Gordon, "Whenever a child decides to communicate with his parent, he does so because he has a need. Always there is something going on inside of him."

Reality check: I've participated in raising two children to responsible adulthood. I remember many, many times when my children were communicating nothing more than *wants* to me and my wife. They didn't *need* anything; they simply *wanted* something. I eventually figured out that a child cannot distinguish between need and want because to a child, they feel the same. It is the responsibility of adults to help children learn to make the distinction, to separate the wheat from the chaff, and that responsibility involves the word "no." In fact, the child *needs* to hear the word "no," and often. That word helps a child grow into a much happier adult. Adults who cannot separate need from want—and we all know adults of that sort—are not happy people. They are chronic malcontents.

Gordon argued that his no-lose approach to parent–child communication empowers kids with a sense of self-worth, and an authoritative approach suffocates it. Need-fulfilled and self-esteem-boosted offspring will appreciate Mom's and Dad's efforts, and a positive feedback loop will form between parent and child. The child, feeling that his parents respect his needs, will respect theirs, and they will respond by respecting his needs even more, and harmony will fill households, spill out into the streets, and flow throughout the world. The theme song for this utopianism was The Fifth Dimension's 1969 hit "Aquarius." It promised a world overflowing with peace, love, and liberation.

Make no mistake, there were plenty of people in the early 1970s, including yours truly, who heard that song and believed in its message, just as we read Gordon's book and believed its message. We drank the utopian Kool-Aid as often as it was offered to us. We were convinced that if we, the Anointed Generation, could make ourselves heard, we would be able to bring closure to history. We would sweep out the old and usher in a reborn, peace-and-love world in which everyone's inner child could come out of hiding and everyone would become the complete human he or she was originally destined to be!

Gordon was a perfect fit with this head-in-the-clouds thinking, prevalent at the time. In his perfect world, the notion of moral absolutes is irrelevant, outdated, even anathema. In his estimation, right and wrong depend on unique aspects of the culture in question and the individual's point of view. It followed that in order to establish the brave new nonjudgmental world that Gordon and others of the time envisioned, the traditional (absolutist) family had to go and children had to be given an equal voice in determining how they were raised. But even more than this, Gordon actually thought that most adults could not be trusted to make good decisions for children. After all, the adults in question had been raised by parents who thought they knew what was best, who imposed authority, who suppressed their children's inner children. Those adults had been contaminated, perhaps irrevocably. Only adults raised the new way, Gordon's way, could be trusted with the new parenting assignment.

Other parents find it difficult to throw off the oppressive value system acquired from their own parents and now causing them to be excessively judgmental and unaccepting of their children . . . using methods of influence not too dissimilar from brainwashing and thought control.

Yes, Gordon is actually comparing parents who use firm discipline to steer their children's character development to dictators such as Joseph Stalin and Idi Amin! He consistently engaged in this sort of over-the-top demonization to make his points. Today, we might read that assertion and chuckle. Certainly, no respectable publisher would publish it. But the times weren't normal. Normal, in fact, was precisely what was wrong; it had to go. Precisely because his point of view *wasn't* normal, America's media and mental health communities helped Gordon's train gain momentum, and American parents hopped on board.

Gordon did graciously grant parents permission to model their values and express their moral beliefs to their children, but that's where he drew the line. He argued that parents should not force their beliefs on their children. Force was anything persuasive, and persuasion was brainwashing and mind control. To go beyond mere modeling and explaining, Gordon asserted, is a violation of the child's civil rights.

> *Why don't parents understand that their sons and daughters are human beings and that* it is human nature to fight for freedom *whenever it is threatened by another? . . . Why don't parents comprehend that civil rights must begin at home?*

Gordon also believed that parent–child relationships would be far better if parents were more open-minded when their children embraced radically different values.

> *It has impressed me to see how many parents in deep trouble in their relationships with their children are persons with very strong and very rigid concepts of what is right and wrong. . . . Parents whose system of values and beliefs is more flexible, more permeable, more amenable to change. . . . These are the parents who find it easier to accept changing patterns of sexual behavior, different styles of clothing, or rebellion against school authority. . . . The beliefs and values of one generation are not necessarily those of the next. . . . Irrational and repressive authority often deserves to be strongly resisted.*

Gordon is most definitely saying that parents need to accept it when their kids become sexually active as young teens, wear provocative clothing, and defy their teachers. It is no coincidence that compared with their 1950s counterparts, today's young teens are much more sexually active, wear far more provocative clothing,

Parent-Babble

and are much more likely to defy their teachers. Gordon opened a Pandora's box.

You might be asking, "But surely Gordon recognizes that there are times when parents must make a unilateral decision and insist that their kids comply, right?" Actually, he does not. He does not think adults are really qualified to make unequivocal decisions on their children's behalf.

Who is to decide what is in the best interest of society? The child? The parent? Who knows best? These are difficult questions and there are dangers in leaving the determination of "best interest" with the parents.

Reality check: Children do *not* know what is in their best interest. That's precisely why they need decisive adult leadership. In effect, Gordon reduces the role of parent to that of being simply a *provider*—of food, clothing, medical care, shelter, transportation, and so on. If one takes Gordon's philosophy to its logical conclusion, children are perfectly capable of directing their own upbringing. Because their feelings are *their* feelings, they will make better decisions for themselves than will their parents and other responsible adults. Really?

Still Alive and Kickin'

Two generations removed, Gordon's parenting philosophy—actually a clarion call for the remaking of society as a whole—may seem no more than an interesting historical blip. The problem is that lots of otherwise intelligent people thought Gordon was who he believed himself to be: a prophet who had unique insight into the problems of the world and

46

how to solve them. Keep in mind that his philosophy fit neatly into the antiauthority, relativistic, progressive mood of the time.

The other thing to consider is that Gordon's views are still very much in vogue with mental health professionals, even those who are too young to know of him. After all, the young people who initially heeded his message are now faculty in most graduate psychology and family counseling programs around the country. Gordon successfully handed his baton to them, and they are handing it on to the next generation of therapists.

Consider child therapy, for example. The efficacy of no form of child therapy—not one!—has ever been demonstrated in controlled studies. The value of a therapist taking a child into an office and playing with the child or talking with him about his feelings and problems is questionable, to say the least. In fact, when a therapist interacts in private with a problem child, the child may well come to believe that the therapist is validating his behavior, in which case the problem will likely worsen. I have heard numerous testimonies of such outcomes—parents lamenting that when they let their kids talk privately to therapists, problems went from bad to much worse. Therapists who ask children how they feel about their parents' rules and expectations and what their parents do when the children disobey are sending those children a Gordonian message: Your feelings should be a significant factor in determining the rules and expectations that govern your life.

An example: Two parents asked for my advice about their eight-year-old son, who still threw wild tantrums when he didn't get his way. In the course of our conversation, they revealed that two years earlier, they had seen a therapist who talked to them and their son separately and then told them the problem was their parenting style. They were dictatorial, they didn't show sufficient respect for their son's point of view, and their son felt like he didn't have a voice in the family. His frequent tantrums were simply expressions of pent-up rage over having to live with two dictators. Whether she realized it or not, this therapist was channeling Thomas Gordon. Her advice to these parents was right out of his playbook.

In the late 1960s and early 1970s, Gordon and others who followed in his footsteps infected America with a virus that is still alive and well. A good number of today's parents, without realizing it, treat their children in ways that bear no resemblance to the manner in which children were raised in the 1950s and before. Those parents might even read this chapter and think Gordon was deluded. They might even ask themselves how any rational person could ever swallow Gordon's advice. Yet in their own families, they negotiate with their kids, they don't feel completely comfortable exercising authority, they think their kids' reactions to decisions they make are valid indicators of whether those decisions are right or wrong, they try to please their children and avoid doing things that might displease them, they allow their kids to call adults by their first names, and their punishments are weak (if they truly punish at all). This is Gordon's legacy. He had an enormous impact on American parenting, an impact from which America is still reeling. Gordon wasn't a blip on the screen; he was the program, and it's still in constant rerun in homes all over America.

Deconstructing Authority Babble

During a break in one of my seminars, a person expressed dismay about some of the things I was saying. He asked, "John, don't you feel that *anything* good came out of the parenting revolution you talk about?"

"This may seem very closed-minded," I said, "But my answer is no, nothing of any value came out of it. Children are worse off, parents are worse off, schools are worse off, and America is worse off."

Then he said, "Well, it's just that you talk as if nothing those folks ever said was right."

"Yes, that's exactly what I mean to say. The research that hadn't been done when they were writing and speaking has now been done, and the research clearly says that nothing they said was right. I know it's very 'incorrect' to say that in the very tolerant world of today, but that's the way it is."

It's difficult to accept that people who were smart enough to write books that became best-sellers were wrong about everything, but after examining the evidence, talking with countless parents, and attempting his methods myself, I've come to the conclusion that Gordon was wrong about everything. For one thing, and perhaps the most important thing, he offered no impartial research to support his claims. He supported most of his contentions with anecdotes based on personal experiences. Since his time, however, a good amount of research into parenting style outcomes has been conducted, and the results do not confirm *anything* Gordon said about the effect of parent authority on children.

In the early 1970s, psychologist Diana Baumrind began what is known as a longitudinal study of parenting outcomes. She interviewed and observed parents and then followed up on them and their kids at periodic intervals. Her research is considered without equal in the parenting field. Based on two primary variables, control and nurturing, Baumrind assigned parents to one of three categories:

- ◆ **Authoritarian parents** are highly controlling, punitive, demand unquestioning obedience, and are most definitely not warm and fuzzy. They don't demonstrate adequate affection toward their kids.

◆ **Authoritative parents** punish misbehavior, but they take the time to explain their actions to their kids. They insist on obedience and respect, but they are highly affectionate toward their children.

◆ **Permissive parents** fit Gordon's description of the ideal. They negotiate conflict with their children (and therefore find themselves in lots of arguments), are wishy-washy about their rules and expectations, and are highly affectionate.

In Baumrind's taxonomy, the authoritative parent is the traditional model. Keep in mind, however, that Gordon made no distinction between authoritative and authoritarian parents. To him, authority was authority, and it was all bad.

Baumrind has consistently found that children of authoritative parents score highest on scales of adjustment and well-being. Compared with children of either authoritarian or permissive parents, they are happier, possess better coping skills, are less prone to emotional difficulties, do better in school, and enjoy better relationships. In other words, Gordon was wrong. Traditional parent authority is good for kids.

The issue of ethics provides another way of contrasting parenting styles. Ethical leaders act in accord with the best interests of the people they are leading; unethical leaders act solely with their own interests in mind. Ethical leaders want what is best for the people they lead; unethical leaders want what is best for themselves. Ethical leaders are trying to help the people they lead improve themselves; unethical leaders want to keep the people they lead in subservient, dependent positions.

When this ethical/unethical distinction is applied to parents, we can conclude that some are ethical and some are unethical. Authoritative parents realize that children need authority that is calmly, consistently, and confidently conveyed, that authority so delivered is as nurturing as love; authoritarian parents impose dogmatic authority because they are threatened by children who are not subservient. The problem with Gordon was that he saw no such distinction. To him, parent authority was bad, period. There was no "good" way of dispensing it.

Good old common sense reveals that Gordon's prescribed model for parent–child conflict resolution is more than foolish. Accordingly, if a child refuses to go to the doctor for treatment of an illness, the parents have no right to make him go. If a child cheats on a math test, the child's teachers and parents have no right to punish him.

Gordon would say that I am making a mockery of his advice, that he would certainly approve of parents making unilateral decisions in certain areas. He said as much in the aforementioned letter he sent to my syndicate in the early 1980s. But he doesn't use words to that effect anywhere in his book. The disciple who "facilitated" the seminar I attended didn't make any such distinction. So how could a parent who read his book or attended one of his seminars make that distinction? How was that parent to know Gordon thinks it's okay, in certain situations, for parents to exercise unilateral authority over a child? He never says so. In fact, he makes numerous statements to the exact opposite effect. The reader can discover, by reading *Parent Effectiveness Training* and *Teaching Children Self-Discipline,* that Gordon never, not once, makes any allowance for the use of unequivocal, unilateral parent authority.

Gordon's philosophy is also internally illogical. Conveniently, he never addresses the issue of what to do if a child decides to reject the notion of democracy altogether. Imagine a ten-year-old child saying, "Mom and Dad, I've come to the conclusion that you both lack decision-making ability, so I've decided that since you won't make final decisions around here, I will. Since you won't insist on obedience from me, I will insist on it from you. Someone needs to be running this show, after all."

How would Gordon suggest that parents deal with this scenario, since they have abdicated all authority and have accepted that they should not judge the child's decisions as wrong? To be consistent with his own philosophy, Gordon would have to accept that the child's desire to be the authority figure in the family is simply an expression of a strong psychological need that the child's parents should respect and accommodate. If one reads Gordon literally, the inescapable conclusion is that these parents have permission to negotiate a power-sharing bargain with the child, but they have absolutely no right to say, "Dream on, kid. You'll run your life when you move out of here and not a day before."

Nature abhors a vacuum; so does authority. When parents abdicate authority, their children will rush to fill the void. I submit that Gordon's legacy is one of the primary reasons why there are so many families in which it's obvious the kids are in charge.

A pediatrician friend of mine related the following true story: He saw a five-year-old girl and her mother for a routine well-child visit during which he noted that the child was scheduled for an immunization. When he indicated such, the child became livid. She turned on her mother and shouted, "You said I wasn't going to get a shot!"

The mother looked sheepish and said, "Has Mommy been bad?"

"Yes!" the girl shouted.

"Does Mommy need a spanking?" the mother asked.

"Yes!"

The mother turned around, bent slightly over, and presented her bottom to the child, who proceeded to spank her in front of my completely astonished, speechless friend. As they say, real life is far stranger than fiction.

I assure you that nothing even remotely resembling that incident ever took place in the pre-Gordon parenting era. As I mentioned in the first chapter, historical accounts of children and teenagers paint a very different picture from what we see today. Children got into mischief, yes; children have always done that. But rarely were they openly defiant and disrespectful toward their parents, teachers, and other authority figures.

History books, diaries, letters, journals, and other materials demonstrated that even very young boys and girls willingly and proudly performed chores, tended to many of their own needs, respected teachers, did their own homework, and even helped support their families financially. All of this helped them grow up to be responsible, sturdy citizens who contributed constructively to society. Those once-upon-a-time kids did not fulfill these responsibilities because they were more capable than today's kids. And they certainly did not behave responsibly and respectfully toward adults because their parents engaged in active listening or "no-lose" methods of conflict resolution. They behaved as they did because their parents expected that of them, without reservation or compromise. Thus, children learned the value of hard work, reliability, responsibility, loyalty to the family, and the need to respect legitimate authority figures such as their parents, teachers, bosses, and the law.

Even today, in non-Western cultures where psychological parenting has not established a foothold, parents expect their children to obey, and the children do. Ironically, in many cultures we describe as "undeveloped" or "developing," parents are much more effective than is generally the case in today's America at raising secure, responsible, happy, loyal, and self-sufficient human beings.

Mind you, there are still a good number of parents in America who have refused to raise their children the new way, who parent much like their great-grandparents did. Their families are parent centered, not child centered. These parents make their expectations clear, and their children do as they are told. They have no tolerance for their children doing less than what they are capable of doing, so their kids do their best. And their kids are happier for all of that. These parenting exceptions prove that the old ways still work for the betterment of child, family, community, and culture.

Reclaiming Authority

If you are ready to start a retro-revolution in your family, you must be clear about your ultimate goal. Knowing your goal—defining it precisely, in terms of specific objectives—will enable you to focus and fine-tune your parenting behavior. In that regard, I propose that the only valid parenting goal is to raise a compassionate, responsible citizen, a good neighbor who will strengthen community and culture.

When I'm doing a small-group workshop, I have each parent write a ten-word-and-phrase description of the adult they want their child to be when the child is thirty years old. That becomes their parenting target. That's what I encourage you to do, right now. That goal—always expressed in terms of "character words" such as *compassionate, charitable, responsible, faithful, hardworking, trustworthy, honest,* and *generous*—becomes a guide for your day-to-day parenting behavior. In any given parenting situation, you simply ask yourself, "Of the options available to me right now, which one will best advance my child toward becoming a responsible, compassionate, charitable adult?" Having a clear goal and keeping the goal in the forefront of your "parent mind" is the key to consistent, purposeful parenting behavior.

Then, recognize that just as soldiers, employees, and church congregations need leadership, so do children. Become a leader of your children!

A parent once told me she didn't feel she was cut out to be a good leader. I told her that only a small minority of adults are cut out to be effective leaders of other adults. But any responsible adult who has a child's best interest in mind can be an effective leader of that child. A child cannot mold his or her character alone. His innate self-serving nature is too strongly embedded. It takes patient, purposeful parent leadership to help a child develop respect for others and a desire to serve. With that in mind, here are the elements of a parenting style that best accomplishes exactly that:

- ◆ *Be decisive.* Don't ask a five-year-old what he wants to eat for supper, where he wants to sleep, when he wants to go to bed, or what his chores and the rules that govern his life should be. Act like you know what you're doing. Wear your authority as if it belongs to you.

- ◆ *Communicate clearly and purposefully.* Say what you mean, and mean what you say. When communicating expectations, use an economy of words. The more words you use, the more you begin to sound as if you are *asking* instead of *telling*.

- ◆ *Delegate responsibility.* By the time a child is four, he should be "earning his keep." He should have daily chores that take precedence over after-school activities. And you should not pay him for doing these chores, no more than he should pay you for fixing his breakfast. He does these chores because that's part of being a member of a family.

◆ *Penalize deliberate misbehavior and irresponsibility.* Do not tolerate disrespect or disobedience, but before or after you punish (depending on when the child is most receptive), explain why you are doing what you're doing and that you really don't like doing it. You simply must—it's your responsibility.

◆ *Have no problem saying, "Because I said so."* That is how you can stay out of nonproductive verbal warfare with your kids. You pay taxes because the government tells you, and it doesn't have to give you a good reason, right? The earlier a child gets used to the fact that everyone has to do things simply because someone else says they have to, the better for all concerned.

◆ *Don't yell, threaten, bribe, beg, or bargain.* Give instructions as if you expect obedience. "It's time for you to pick up these toys" is far more likely to result in compliance than, "My friend Mrs. Jones is coming over, and we'd like to use this room. So would you do Mommy a favor and pick up these toys for me? Okay?"

◆ *Understand and accept that your children will misbehave.* When it happens, there's no need to freak out or overreact. Simply deal with it. Reprimand firmly but without yelling, correct without criticizing, and punish in ways that establish permanent memories but not resentment.

◆ *Stand confidently at center stage in your family.* Understand that you cannot exercise effective leadership if your children don't pay attention to you. Make it clear to your kids that most of the attention in your family goes from child to parent, not parent to child.

For more specifics concerning this prescription, I refer the reader to my book *The Well-Behaved Child: Discipline That REALLY Works!* In it, I describe what effective parent authority looks like—its essential ingredients—and give real-life examples of solutions to behavior problems that range from garden variety to very strange indeed.

Self-Esteem Babble

*"It used to be about trying to do something;
now it's about trying to be somebody."*

—Meryl Streep, playing Margaret Thatcher
in *The Iron Lady*

I often conduct a very revealing exercise with my parent audiences around the country. I begin by asking, "How many of you believe that high self-esteem is a good thing and parents should do all they can to help their children acquire it?" In an audience of, say, 500, at least 450 hands go up. (When I look around, the folks who are not raising their hands are usually my age and older.)

I then say, "Now, raise your hand again if you'd prefer to live next door to a person with high self-esteem as opposed to someone who is humble and modest." Not one hand has ever gone up. Mind you, I've conducted this exercise hundreds of times.

"Okay then, raise your hand if you'd prefer to work for someone with high self-esteem as opposed to someone who is humble and modest." Again, no hands go up.

"Well then, raise your hand if you'd rather be close friends with a person with high self-esteem as opposed to a person who is humble and modest." Same result.

At that point, I say, "I could go through a comprehensive list of relationships. In each case, you would tell me you'd rather be in relationship with a person who is humble and modest. Isn't that fascinating, especially in light of the fact that nearly all of you said you believe high self-esteem is a good thing for children to possess."

I go on to explain that their response to the first question reflected what they've heard on television from talking heads and celebrity talk-show people, as well as what they've read in books, newspapers, and magazines. High self-esteem has been promoted as both a personal ideal and the brass ring of parenting since around 1970. It has since become almost as American as Mom and apple pie. In 1986, the governor of California even signed legislation creating the California Task Force to Promote Self-Esteem and Personal and Social Responsibility. The expectation was that higher levels of self-esteem would reduce teen pregnancy, crime, the dropout rate, drug use, and a host of other social problems, saving the state huge amounts of money. (None of the money spent by the task force resulted in one identifiable benefit.) The notion that high self-esteem is desirable has become "common knowledge," so when I ask whether self-esteem is good for kids, everyone says yes. But then I ask questions that tap common *sense* (i.e., intuition), not common knowledge, and everyone suddenly realizes that self-esteem isn't all it's been made out to be.

And just to correct a widespread misunderstanding, the opposite of high self-esteem is not depression or a general feeling of worthlessness and incompetence. In fact, researchers have discovered that people with high self-esteem are highly prone to depression, especially when their lives take a sour turn. Generally speaking, they have great difficulty coping with adversity. It seems that depression may be a likely *consequence* of high self-esteem—not its opposite.

As reflected in part two of the aforementioned poll, the actual converse of high self-esteem is humility and modesty. Those are classical ideals. A prideful sense of self is not. Once upon a not-so-long-ago time in America and most of the world, people with high self-esteem—although the idiom wasn't even in use—were regarded as what my mother called boors. That's an old-fashioned term referring to a person who lacks social grace, brags of his accomplishments, tries to be the center of attention, and is insensitive to others—a self-absorbed narcissist, in other words. When boors engage in conversation, they want to talk about themselves. On the other hand, humble people are socially gracious and courteous. They are interested in you and look for opportunities to assist you. Oh, and by the way, *humble* and *introverted* are not synonymous. That's another misunderstanding. Most humble people are very comfortable in social situations. They simply don't want to be the center of attention. From all accounts, George Washington was a humble man. He certainly wasn't a wallflower.

The fact that high self-esteem should not be a personal or cultural ideal is clear to me because I am a member of the last generation of American children who were not *allowed* to possess high self-esteem. When a child in the 1950s had an outburst of high self-esteem—a self-expansive moment of calling attention to himself in some showy fashion—one of his parents would snap his or her fingers and say sternly, "You're acting too big for your britches. You'd better size yourself to those britches or I'm gonna size you to 'em. What's it gonna be?" Invariably, the child sized himself. Kids in my generation also remember being told to get down off our high horses. That meant we were showing off, blowing our own horns, bragging about our accomplishments, and that it would be in our best interest if we stopped, immediately.

Throughout the Bible, warnings are given about high self-esteem. In the Book of Proverbs, for example, one finds a clear warning to those who "exalt themselves." They will be abased, the author says, meaning it's only a matter of time before they are brought down. In the Sermon on the Mount, Jesus blesses the "meek and the poor in spirit." It's clear he was not referring to people who think highly of themselves. My point is that humility was regarded as a virtue for thousands of years before high self-esteem shoved it aside in the 1970s.

In slightly less than two generations, the classical ideals of humility and modesty have been replaced by the nouveau notion that an elevated opinion of oneself and one's abilities and accomplishments is a desirable characteristic. Again, the problem is modern psychology and some of its most public champions: so-called parenting experts. High self-esteem is one of the monkey wrenches they threw into America's works.

From Common Sense to Corruption

The concept of self-esteem has its roots in the positive psychology movement that began in the 1950s, largely in reaction to Freud's emphasis on pathology. The new movement's pioneer was psychologist and Brandeis University professor Abraham Maslow (1908–1970), who coined the term *self-actualized* to describe a person who had realized his or her full potential for creative living. Maslow did not have children in mind, however. He thought that a self-actualized state was really not possible until one was well along in years and able to look back with satisfaction on his or her life.

Maslow referred to two different sources of personal affirmation: respect from others (positive recognition, acceptance, status, appreciation) and esteem from within (the feeling that one is a decent person, capable of playing a valuable role in society). According to Maslow, a person who lacks the latter—which he called self-esteem (it had previously been called self-respect)—will be driven neurotically (in self-defeating ways) to acquire it and will be unable to achieve self-actualization. It is significant to note that Maslow's definition of self-esteem was not radical. He simply assigned a new term to what is called "being comfortable in one's own skin."

Maslow's theory inspired a number of new humanistic therapies, most notably Carl Rogers's client-centered therapy. Rogers (1902–1987) believed humans were innately good. He taught his students that people who sought psychological help need unconditional acceptance, personal validation, and understanding of their feelings, as opposed to negative judgment of their thoughts, attitudes, and actions. Once again, Rogers was not proposing anything new. He was simply saying that people who think they are capable will act in capable ways. That's common sense.

It's difficult to tell exactly who was primarily responsible for moving the term *self-esteem* into the vernacular, but psychotherapist Nathaniel Branden is the prime suspect. In 1969, in *The Psychology of Self-Esteem*, Branden defined *self-esteem* as "the disposition to experience oneself as competent to cope with the basic challenges of life and as worthy of happiness." He proposed that this personal belief was the keystone of psychological health. In his view, a person who lacks self-esteem is vulnerable to all manner of emotional turmoil and social difficulties. Note that Branden's definition, like Maslow's, was not radical in the least. His use of the term described the American spirit of tenacity, hard work, and optimism.

Ultimately, the problem was a function of the term itself. To *esteem* means to have a high opinion of and admire someone. So, despite the fact that Maslow, Rogers, and Branden did not say that healthy people possess a prideful opinion of themselves or admire themselves, they used a term that connotes that very meaning, greatly increasing the chances that the term would be corrupted, as it was. Perhaps if they had used a familiar term such as *self-respect,* which is really what they were talking about, the ensuing problems might not have occurred, or at least not to the same degree. But the term *self-respect* was already in use, and psychologists like to come up with new words because new words imply new ideas, and that's what psychologists like to think they're inventing.

Maslow, Rogers, and Branden certainly laid the groundwork for America's love affair with self-esteem, but it was another 1960s mental health professional, family counselor Dorothy Briggs, who introduced the concept to American parents. By turns a teacher and school psychologist, Briggs shared the view then becoming popular among so-called helping professionals that because of the destructive nature of their own unenlightened upbringing, American parents were ill equipped to rear children properly. Instead of the historically sound family model that placed parents and their expectations at the defining center of the family universe, Briggs advocated child-centered families in which children's feelings and psychological needs were of foremost concern. She thought, as did Thomas Gordon, that the traditional exercise of parental authority damaged children's psyches. It's important to understand that Briggs did not think that only *some* parents needed her re-education program; *all* parents did. She thought that American parenting was and always had been destructive to children.

Proceeding strictly on the basis of her opinions, gleaned solely from personal experience, Briggs deemed American parenting hopelessly broken and fancied herself as one of its saviors. She launched her mission in the late 1950s by leading parent education courses in which she taught parents radically new methods for raising children and resolving parent–child conflict. In the mid-1960s, she became Thomas Gordon's first certified Parent Effectiveness Training instructor. At that point, under Gordon's tutelage, her influence began to expand rapidly. In 1970, she published what quickly became the scripture of self-esteem–based parenting: *Your Child's Self-Esteem*. In it, Briggs taught that self-esteem is a child's greatest need, the key to happiness and success. She proclaimed that the child so endowed "has it made." Her book quickly won praise from the mental health community. Along with Gordon's *Parent Effectiveness Training* and psychologist Haim Ginott's *Between Parent and Child* (to be discussed in the next chapter), it marked the dawning of a new era in American parenting, one that the overwhelming majority of psychologists, counselors, and therapists of the day believed would produce happier, healthier children. Unfortunately, the evidence shows otherwise. As the reader will see, the national effort to instill high self-esteem in children has been a resounding flop.

According to Briggs, the cause of nearly all of society's ills— crime, deviant behavior, sexual promiscuity, substance abuse, and so on—is low self-esteem. A person who engages in antisocial or self-destructive behavior is actually a victim who, as a child, developed "negative reflections" about himself. These harmful self-beliefs were acquired through childhood exposure to a toxic adult—most likely a punitive parent or a critical teacher—who failed to make him feel worthwhile and deserving of love.

Like Gordon, Briggs stressed that a child's feelings were more important than his or her behavior. She believed that a child can learn "proper" behavior (as defined by parental expectations) without developing the sense that he is a person of fundamental worth. The critical issue, therefore, is not how the child acts, but how the child feels about himself privately. Seen from Briggs's perspective, "good" behavior can be nothing more than a mask a child wears to conceal inner pain, and "bad" behavior is merely a symptom of an unmet need or a child's way of expressing the damage done to him by parents who insist that he comply with their expectations.

Briggs's prescription for developing high self-esteem in children included liberal amounts of praise, affirmations, and positive experiences. Like Gordon, she promoted democratic families, demonized parent authority, and firmly opposed punishment in any form, for any misbehavior. The only real difference between her book and Gordon's was her emphasis on self-esteem, which Gordon talked about but did not develop as fully.

How to Damage a Child Without Really Trying

According to Briggs, it is essential that parents strive to see the world through their children's eyes and allow them to freely express both positive and negative reactions to events and experiences. Forcing a child to repress negative feelings causes the child to think that because the feelings are bad, *he* is bad as well. In this way, parents annihilate the child's sense of self-worth.

I happen to agree with Briggs that there is great value in parental empathy, the ability of parents to put themselves mentally into their children's shoes and have understanding and compassion for the struggles they must go through in order to grow into responsible people of character. I also agree that parents should be prudent in how they speak to and act toward their children. Their words and actions should always be driven by love and a desire to properly mold their children's character, not by frustration or anger. However, none of those considerations preclude a parent from communicating clear intolerance of (including the punishment of) tantrums, disobedience, disrespect, aggression, lying, stealing, and other misbehavior. Patience and tolerance only go so far.

Briggs disapproves of parents saying anything negative to a child. To say, "I don't like messy rooms" is okay, but to say "I've lost my patience over the messy way you keep your room. It's very disrespectful of you. So, I've decided that whether you clean it or not, you're not going out with your friends tonight. Furthermore, from this point on, your privileges depend on a clean, orderly room" is not okay. Briggs believes that even the slightest verbal correction or restrictive or punitive discipline is likely to result in emotional harm. In essence, Briggs warns parents against doing anything that causes a child to feel even the slightest twinge of emotional discomfort. That might make the child feel guilty, and guilt negates the child's right to a positive, natural sense of self. The child supposedly translates his parents' disapproval thus: "I am bad because I did something bad."

In fact, guilt is a perfectly functional emotion, necessary to maintaining civilized society. It is dysfunctional only at the extremes of the guilt scale. At one extreme are people who are incapable of feeling guilt, no matter how damaging their actions toward others are. That is the defining characteristic of a narcissistic sociopath, whose ultimate goal is to gain advantage over others. At the other end of the guilt spectrum are people who are burdened with frequent, often incapacitating feelings of unwarranted guilt. That defines neurosis. But in between those extremes are people who, when they do bad things that cause other people unnecessary discomfort or distress, feel bad about what they have done. Guilt drives valid repentance, apology, atonement, and restitution. If I speak in a thoughtlessly abrasive manner to my wife, for example, I seek her forgiveness *because* I feel guilt. My transgression causes her emotional distress; therefore, because I care deeply for her, it causes *me* emotional distress as well. Without that guilt capacity, I can justify my abrasiveness, and things will go downhill from there.

Let's face it, we all do self-centered things. Self-centeredness is a lifelong affliction. The healthy person recognizes that potential and strives to control it to the best of his ability. If he succeeds, his relationships improve accordingly, as does his self-respect. Adults are capable of facing that struggle. A healthy adult is capable of feeling regretful about a self-centered act directed toward someone else. Children, however, are not independently capable of facing that struggle, of experiencing that regret. This is one of the things, in fact, that differentiates child from valid adult. When children do self-serving things that cause discomfort and distress to others, they need adult agents in their lives who will cause them to feel the regret—yes, the guilt—that drives apology and restitution. This should not be done through emotional outburst. It should be done by a parent or parents sitting down with an offending child and telling him forcefully but clearly why what he did was wrong, why he should feel shame, why he needs to make apology and restitution in one form or another, and why they must punish him (although there are times when "the talk" will be punishment enough). This is an essential parent responsibility.

It is ironic that although the self-esteem crowd had a problem with parents causing children to feel guilt, they had no problem whatsoever making parents feel guilty for being anything less than positive and affirming toward their children. And parents certainly did feel guilty. Because I've been a contrarian voice since the early 1980s, parents feel they can tell me about their experiences with the parenting philosophy espoused by people such as Briggs and Gordon. Indeed, I often hear the word *guilty*, as in "I just always felt guilty for what I did in reaction to my child's misbehavior or for how I really felt about it." These are parents who never felt comfortable with the new marching orders but tried their best to follow the beat out of fear that if they didn't, they would do irreversible harm to their kids. Never before in the history of any culture have parents felt such incapacitating self-doubt. This is the mess Gordon and Briggs and others left behind.

The Truth Comes Out

For four decades and counting, mental health professionals have been serving self-esteem Kool-Aid to parents who have every reason to believe that people with impressive capital letters after their names know what they're talking about. By the 1980s, a parent who still practiced traditional authoritative parenting, who insisted on respect and obedience from his or her kids, was likely to be seen as an unenlightened throwback by neighbors, friends, teachers, school administrators, school counselors, therapists, and even relatives. Parents, especially women, began to experience tremendous peer and social pressure to conform to the new parenting ethic, and most of them did just that. Mothers began to believe that their primary responsibility was to protect their children from any and all forms of psychological insult. Making that attempt has seriously deflated the authority of the American mother.

Initially, fathers did not buy into this new parenting enterprise, but the American dad has definitely become more feeling and relationship oriented of late. Some social critics are even saying that fathers have become more "feminized." In effect, many children live with two mommies, says sociologist David Blankenhorn, author of *Fatherless America*. One of these mommies is biologically female; the other is biologically male. In other words, many children have very dedicated fathers; the problem is they lack traditional male role models. I attribute this to a slow but sure shift in the American father's point of view from long-term character-based goals (like instilling a positive work ethic) to more immediate feelings-based goals. This is an unfortunate trend, one that is not in the best interest of children of either gender. Furthermore, as with his wife, the authority of the American father has been considerably reduced.

Male children need masculine fathers who expect them to be responsible, to always do their best. Female children need masculine fathers who inspire them, when they reach adulthood, to seek responsible men who always do their best. Children don't need fathers who try to be their most emotionally sensitive buddies.

Like Gordon, Briggs was recommending what I call "therapeutic parenting." I'm referring to a parenting style that puts more emphasis on cultivating and protecting a child's pristine feeling state than on shaping his or her character, one that emphasizes relationship over leadership, one in which parent and child are essentially peers. Like Gordon, Briggs was a proponent of the democratic family. At one point in her book, she even makes this statement: "Democracy in government has little meaning to a child unless he feels the daily benefits of it at home."

That's simply wrong. There is no evidence that the architects of the greatest democracy in history were reared in democratic families by parents who were focused on helping them "feel good about themselves" and gave them an equal voice in family matters. Reading their biographies, one is struck by the humility of George Washington, Thomas Jefferson, John Adams, James Madison, and

Abraham Lincoln. It is clear that they were not motivated by the promise of public acclaim or fortune, but by the desire to improve the lot of all Americans. These were men who felt the call to serve. Furthermore, all accounts of their childhoods indicate that they respected and obeyed their parents, and not because their parents gave them proper explanations or went to pains to never tarnish their feelings, but simply because their parents expected their complete obedience. The aforementioned Great Americans were the beneficiaries, not the victims, of their parents' authority. Were they fully capable of thinking for themselves? Of course they were! Did they grow up to be emotional cripples? Of course not! When looked at through the lens of history, Briggs's and Gordon's claims for self-esteem and family democracy are nothing short of ludicrous.

In the 368 pages that make up *Your Child's Self-Esteem,* Briggs makes no reference to any sound research that might lend credibility to her assertions. She provides no scientifically supported confirmation of her claim that traditional, authoritative parenting produces insecure, other-dependent children who are ill equipped to function in society. She presents no evidence to support her idea that punishment, even when lovingly applied, destroys a child's sense of self-worth and leads to a life marked by unhealthy relationships. She puts forth no objective research confirming that children from democratic families emerge from childhood and adolescence emotionally healthier than those raised by parents who know best. She presents no evidence supporting the contention that high self-esteem is the key to a successful life. She presented no such evidence because she couldn't. At the time, no one had done research into any of those issues. But the research results are now in, and they indicate that Briggs could not have been more off base.

Research done since 1990 clearly indicates that although people with high self-esteem do indeed "feel good about themselves," they have generally low regard for others. The relationship appears to be what economists call a zero-sum equation: As esteem for one's self goes up, regard for others goes down. In other words, the two do not coexist. One either has high self-esteem or has high regard for others, the essence of humility. You don't need a college degree to realize that strong communities and culture depend largely on people who have high regard for others, not on people who think of themselves first.

People with high self-esteem want others to pay attention to them and do things for them. People with high regard for others pay attention to others, looking for opportunities to render courtesies and assistance—simple but meaningful things such as opening doors, helping carry things, giving up their seats, and saying "please" and "thank you." Who would you rather be in relationship with? Who would you rather have as a neighbor, employee, employer, friend, sibling, or spouse? I bet I know your answers, and the research agrees with you!

From 1970 to 2000, more than fifteen thousand articles were written by various scholars, all claiming that high self-esteem was linked to all manner of positive outcomes. In 2003, the Association for Psychological Science asked professor Roy Baumeister of Florida State University to review this body of literature. He concluded that, for the most part, the research was badly flawed: Only two hundred of the fifteen thousand studies met his rigorous criteria. After reviewing those two hundred, Baumeister concluded that high self-esteem did not live up to its press. It did not improve grades or career achievement, lower alcohol use, or reduce violence. In fact, he found that highly aggressive, violent people tend to think very highly of themselves. Baumeister, a former believer in high self-esteem, is quoted as saying that his own findings were "the biggest disappointment of my career."

Most surprising is Baumeister's finding that highly aggressive individuals, including violent criminals, have a very high opinion of themselves. These findings hit the mental health community like a bombshell because until then it had embraced the politically correct notion that criminals were acting out low self-esteem. In other words, well-done research found that the high self-esteem movement was not reducing crime; it was helping to increase it!

I've spoken to a number of people who work in prisons or with criminals. These folks have included parole officers, prison guards, and criminal defense lawyers. Their personal experiences affirm these findings. One Louisiana prison guard I spoke with said, "My job is dangerous exactly because the inmates I guard all have high self-esteem." An Ohio parole officer told me, "None of the criminals I've ever worked with has had low self-esteem." In this regard, it is also significant to note that since public schools jumped on the self-esteem bandwagon with both bureaucratic feet, bullying has increased to the point where it is one of the biggest problems today's teachers and administrators deal with.

Baumeister and researcher Jean Twenge of the University of California have independently discovered that people with high self-esteem possess an inflated sense of self-importance and ability. They think of themselves as more intelligent, talented, likable, admirable, praiseworthy, and all-around awesome than the average person. In short, they think they're a cut above you and me. Their self-image is rarely in line with the actual truth about themselves, however, so it tends to be fragile and easily threatened. When other people or circumstances fail to confirm their inflated self-image, one of two responses is likely: aggression or depression. They either lash out, verbally or physically, or they go into emotional tailspins.

Those reactions are predicted by psychology's flight-or-fight principle, which posits that in response to threat, some folks flee and others fight. So schoolyard bullies, wife beaters, and others with short fuses have high self-esteem (when their inflated self-images are threatened, they fight), but so do some people who experience periodic bouts of depression or debilitating anxiety (when their inflated self-images are threatened, they flee).

The self-esteem crowd said high self-esteem would increase academic achievement, so schools took up the cause. Teachers were sent to workshops in which they learned how to help children feel good about themselves by dispensing copious amounts of praise, even when performance didn't merit it. Instead of using grades to give children accurate feedback about their performance and progress, schools began using grades therapeutically, to boost self-esteem. As a consequence, grade inflation set in, and grades became irrelevant. Kids in the early elementary grades were given exercises in finishing sentences such as, "I'm really special because _____" and making lists of personal characteristics they took pride in. Many schools banned competitive activities such as dodgeball and tetherball from the playground on the belief that losing at games causes children to lose self-esteem.

All of these therapeutic efforts have been for naught. The promise that high self-esteem would boost academic performance hasn't panned out. When children realized they could make good grades without much effort, academic performance suffered. This is reflected in the steady decline of academic achievement levels since 1970. In fact, people with high self-esteem tend to perform *below* their ability level. Because they think anything they do is worthy of merit, they consistently do less than what they are capable of. An illustration comes from the results of a math competition participated in by students from all over the world. According to the Brown Center, a Washington think tank, only 6 percent of South Korean eighth graders expressed confidence in their math skills, compared with 39 percent of eighth graders in the United States. But on an international math assessment, South Korean students scored far ahead of students from the United States. It is significant to note that humility and modesty are still virtues in South Korea.

I have one significant disagreement with Baumeister. He distinguishes between earned and unearned self-esteem. The former, he says, is acquired legitimately, through valid high achievement. On the other hand, a person acquires the latter by being given unearned praise and reward. This distinction is echoed by psychologist Martin Seligman, a former president of the American Psychological Association, who expressed general disenchantment with self-esteem theory in a 2004 interview. Seligman was quoted as saying, "What I think has gone wrong . . . is that we now think we should inject self-esteem directly into our young people, as opposed to producing warranted self-esteem, which I believe comes from doing well with people you love, doing well in sports, and doing well in school."

I think both Baumeister and Seligman are trying not to be controversial. They're pulling their punches in the name of professional correctness. As a result, they end up taking a middle-of-the-road position that can't be defended logically. For example, if it's true that high self-esteem is good and valid only if earned through high accomplishment in some area, that puts people who are disabled mentally or physically at a distinct self-esteem disadvantage. If high self-esteem is a wonderful thing, then should it not be equally available to all regardless of IQ, creativity, or athletic ability?

My position is that no one should think highly of himself or herself, whether "warranted" or not. The most functional people, the best citizens, the most contented people, are those who think highly of *others*, whether those others "warrant" it or not by virtue of accomplishment in some area. That describes people who embody the classical ideal of humility and modesty. I do agree with Seligman that parents and schools have tried to "inject" self-esteem into kids by shielding them from failure, pumping them full of unwarranted praise, running interference for them, and creating artificial success experiences, and that this effort has backfired. But it's important in this regard to keep in mind that parents and schools have been guilty of this because they were grossly misled by the very mental health community that Seligman represents.

In a 2011 article titled "How to Land Your Kid in Therapy," psychologist Lori Gottlieb reported the result of having studied adults in her practice who struggled with stress, anxiety, and depression but who had grown up in loving families. She found that many of their parents had showered them with undeserved praise, had solved their problems (enabled), and had been generally permissive, all in the overarching attempt to ensure their children's happiness. Gottlieb concluded that parents who center their lives on their children and focus on eliminating any negative experience in their lives do more harm than good.

She went on to note that many college professors and administrators report ever-increasing numbers of emotionally fragile students, young people who can't cope with challenge, adversity, failure, and disappointment because their parents tried to protect them from those realities, and they did an admirable job of doing so. In other words, these young people can't handle independence because with independence inevitably comes personal responsibility, challenge, adversity, failure, and disappointment—all things they never learned to deal with or accept. They lack good coping skills because their parents did all the coping for them for the first eighteen or so years of their lives.

Gottlieb's conclusions reminded me of a nineteen-year-old young woman whose mother had micromanaged every aspect of her life before sending her off to college. Her mother had shared her homework responsibilities all the way through grade school and high school, managed her social life, managed her activity schedule, and generally handled every problem that ever came along. The young lady graduated from high school with honors, went to a fairly prestigious college, and promptly had what is generically called a nervous breakdown. She ceased functioning altogether, began having crying spells that lasted hours, dropped out of school, and went back home. It's anyone's best guess when, or even *whether*, she will ever be able to resume her education. This is the price all too many young people are paying for having enabling parents who were doing only what the self-esteem crowd said they should do.

Keep in mind that Baumeister, Twenge, and Gottlieb have only rediscovered the truth of what wise men wrote down 2,000 to 2,500 years ago. They warned against having a high opinion of oneself and said that those who fell into that trap would eventually be abased, or brought down from their high horse. Didn't someone once say there was nothing new under the sun?

The evidence that high self-esteem is toxic to person, relationships, community, and culture has been mounting since the early 1990s. Has it made a difference? Not that I can see. Psychologists still talk about self-esteem like it's a desirable personal attribute, and schools still strive to promote it.

In a documentary I recently watched, a scientist said that people in his field, including himself, had once believed one way, but research had convinced them they were wrong. That's an example of professional ethics at work. When you're wrong, you admit it. I seriously doubt that movers and shakers in the mental health community will ever admit they were wrong about high self-esteem. I think they're hoping that it just fades away into relative obscurity, like so many other theories of human nature that have come and gone over the years, and that the public will be too distracted to notice that some other theory has taken its place. The problem is that if history is any lesson, the next theory isn't going to be worth a hill of beans either.

What About Praise?

The leading researcher on the impact of praise on performance is psychologist Carol Dweck, who did seminal research into praise while on the faculty at Columbia University. Dweck discovered that children praised for being smart actually perform below their ability levels. They also tend to avoid taking on challenges unless they've already proven their competency at them. Dweck discriminates between praising a child for intelligence and praising a child for effort. Praising effort appears to produce good results, but not praising for ability.

Interestingly enough, Dweck found that even when parents are made aware of the results of her study, they keep right on telling their kids how smart they are. Baumeister's findings suggest this may be due to parents taking personal pride in their children's achievements. This pride is so strong that when parents praise their kids, they're "not that far from praising themselves." Baumeister has found that for college students on the verge of failing in class, praise causes their grades to go even further down, not up.

After conducting a series of studies to investigate children's perceptions of praise, psychologist Wulf-Uwe Meyer concluded that by age twelve, children believe that when teachers dispense praise, it's a sign the child in question actually lacks ability and needs encouragement to do better. Meyer also found that teens discount the value of praise even more. They actually value criticisms from teachers more than they do praise, believing that criticism is a more accurate reflection of positive belief in their ability.

The upshot of all this is that, once again, the mental health community was wrong. In and of itself, praise is not necessarily a good thing. Given indiscriminately, as "experts" have told teachers to do, praise is corrosive. Given specifically and focused on effort rather than ability, praise can be helpful in limited doses. But so can criticism.

In order to improve in any performance area, a person must be given accurate feedback. When the person's performance is below what he's capable of, he needs to be told this, straightforwardly. Such feedback isn't necessarily negative. As Meyer's research has shown, it can have a positive effect.

In the final analysis, research simply demonstrates that when adults tell children the truth in constructive fashion, whether the truth is that they put forth admirable effort or that they didn't do as well as they could have, children improve. Again, research confirms common sense.

"But I Want My Child to Be Confident!"

We have arrived at the dominant concern expressed by parents when I take aim at the self-esteemers (which is what I'm going to call them from now on): the fear that if they don't promote high self-esteem by putting their kids at the center of attention, praising them for everything they do, and creating success experiences, their kids won't possess a confident attitude toward life's challenges. Here are three points in response:

◆ There is no evidence whatsoever that humility and modesty are incompatible with the belief that one is capable of dealing adequately with life's challenges. However, there is plenty of evidence that people with high self-esteem underperform, are emotionally vulnerable, and lack adequate coping skills.

◆ People with high self-esteem tend to overestimate their abilities and are highly desirous of attention and approval. They are therefore inclined to engage in risky behavior, such as driving cars at breakneck speeds in order to impress their friends. Good judgment and high self-esteem don't seem to go together.

◆ There is extensive evidence that as American parents adopted self-esteem theory, children have become less confident, more dependent, and less willing to face challenge. This is reflected in many statistics, including the fact that in the forty years between 1970 and 2010, the average age of final, successful emancipation by children from their parents has risen sharply. This does not speak to a generally confident attitude on the part of America's young people.

In summary, the most credible recent research, along with a wagonload of sociological evidence, suggests that a focus on producing high self-esteem in America's children has hurt rather than helped them. It has caused numerous problems and solved none. It has hindered maturity, set back achievement, contributed to an increase in juvenile crime, exacerbated bullying, and caused emotional difficulties that would not have existed otherwise.

Recovery

So what approach should parents use? The answer is simple: Go back to what worked before the self-esteemers began babbling. Most parents aim to raise a child who is confident, secure, and happily at peace with himself or herself. What history and research teach us is that such qualities are not produced by what Briggs, Gordon, and the other new parenting prophets prescribed.

America needs parents who teach children that the truly good life is about what they contribute, not what they gain. Parents need to stop worrying so much about how their children feel and start focusing more on how they treat others—their social behavior. They should expect their children to live according to a set of pro-family and pro-community values, and they must not be afraid to lovingly and authoritatively discipline them to be sure they do so.

Respect for oneself comes from knowing that one is capable of making a valued contribution to the lives of others. That begins with proper manners, family chores, and parents who expect children to do their best, regardless of ability.

It's not complicated; old-fashioned stuff never is. The rules listed at the end of chapter two would be a good place to start.

Punishment Babble

"All pain is a punishment, and every punishment
is inflicted for love as much as for justice."

—JOSEPH-MARIE DE MAISTRE

Punishment is another word that causes much gnashing of teeth among the self-esteem crowd. I once shared a stage with Adele Faber, the author (with Elaine Mazlish) of *How to Talk So Kids Will Listen & Listen So Kids Will Talk.* Faber was a disciple of psychologist Haim Ginott (1922–1973), who published *Between Parent and Child* in 1965. Like Gordon's, Ginott's parenting approach was based on the idea that proper parent communication would prevent most problems and solve those that did occur. He also put more emphasis on feelings than behavior and believed that although consequences should be imposed when children misbehave deliberately, they should be logical or natural. For example, if a child fails to bring his laundry down to the laundry room on time, his laundry doesn't get done that week, and he wears wrinkled clothes. Logical and natural consequences do not include punishments such as being grounded for failing to keep one's room clean and orderly or having to write sentences for disrespecting one's mother.

During the panel discussion, an audience member asked Faber what she thought of my parenting philosophy. Instead of doing the gracious thing and politely refusing to answer the question, she dropped her head, shook it from side to side, looked up to the heavens for inspiration, and after all this drama, said, "Oh, John Rosemond! Oh, John Rosemond! Why oh why are you so hung up on punishment?"

It was rhetorical, of course. She wasn't asking me a question, and I didn't attempt an answer. She went on to talk about how punishment destroyed self-esteem, caused children to feel debilitating shame and guilt, and made them feel fundamentally unworthy. The implication was that I did not understand or even *like* children and wanted only their slavish obedience.

When Faber finished her impassioned speech, an audience member stepped to the microphone and said it would only be fair to give me the opportunity to comment on her parenting philosophy. Would I?

"Yes, I will," I said. "I am from Mars; Ms. Faber is from Venus," and left it at that. I definitely got more laughs than she did.

The truth is that I have my feet on the ground. Faber does not. Her head is in a cloud of romantic fantasy about children. To her, children are pure beings of holy light sent from heaven to grace us with their immaculate presence, and if it weren't for the stupid and mean things adults often do, they would remain unspoiled forever, and we would all be living in an earthly paradise, la, la, la. I am quick to recognize that fantasy in someone else because I've been there, done that.

From Faber's perspective, anyone who believes children should be punished when they misbehave with intent is "hung up" on punishment. In truth, if I am hung up on anything, it is helping children grow up to be responsible, compassionate citizens—good neighbors. Accomplishing that requires responsible adults who help children overcome the innate difficulty they have accepting responsibility for things they do that cause other people discomfort, inconvenience, and distress. Children are masters at passing the buck, masters of denying, blaming, and creating personal soap operas in which they are victims of forces beyond their influence. These traits emerge as soon as children can use language cleverly—by age three. That is why parents use the term *drama queen* to describe many a three-year-old girl. In that context, punishment assigns responsibility in a way that is inescapable. A ten-year-old boy may deny he threw the rock that broke his neighbor's window, but he cannot deny that he is spending a couple of weeks confined to his room because of it.

Punishment also reduces the likelihood of recidivism. After serving his time, that ten-year-old is unlikely to throw rocks at other people's houses ever again. I think we can all agree that it is in the best interest of the ten-year-old to nip his prankishness in the bud. He will be a better person for it. I also maintain that trying to discover the underlying message of his rock throwing—what emotional conflict is he trying to discharge by throwing rocks at people's houses?—isn't going to work. In fact, such an exercise, which is the sort of thing the new parenting prophets recommended, will only *increase* the chance of his doing damage to someone else's house.

Finally, when someone commits a crime, justice is not served unless the person committing the act experiences punishment. That understanding has been an integral part of human social organization since it began. For our purposes, the "crimes" in question are deliberate misbehaviors perpetrated by children. Helping children understand how the world works—an adult obligation—requires that when they misbehave or are purposefully irresponsible, adults who love them punish them. That becomes even more essential when the misbehavior or irresponsibility in question has resulted in emotional or material cost to others.

If those beliefs indicate that I am hung up on punishment, then I stand guilty as charged, and proud of it.

Rejecting Discipline

Consistently, parenting experts who had their roots in the psychological parenting revolution of the 1960s and 1970s demonized punishment. The idea that it's sometimes okay for a child to experience a natural or logical consequence of breaking a rule or being irresponsible is as far as they went. That's consistent with everything else they said. After all, punishment is something done by authority figures, and none of these experts were comfortable with parents exercising authority over children. Parents were teachers, facilitators, mentors, guides, and coaches, but the new prophets did not believe that parents should tell children what to do in no uncertain terms and enforce punitive consequences if they disobey. The use of punishment is demeaning and makes it more likely that the misbehavior will continue. In *Between Parent and Child,* Haim Ginott says:

> *The trouble with techniques that use the parent's power is that they are often not effective when the parent is gone. A child who has been punished for certain behaviors may merely make sure not to do that behavior when the parent is around. . . . The best responses to children's behavior help*

the child behave better because they want to, because of some internal standard.

The notion that a child who is punished for something might take the misbehavior underground—that he will continue to do it when his parents aren't looking—is impossible to refute because some children do exactly that. But children are likely to try and get away with things their parents have told them not to do *even if their parents have never punished them.* Merely telling a child, "I don't want you to do that," is often enough to stimulate his or her mischievous nature.

As for Ginott's comment about a child behaving properly because of an "internal standard," he is at least partly correct. The goal of parent discipline, including punishment, should be to reach a point where the discipline is no longer needed because the child has internalized his parents' values and acts accordingly. Ginott is wrong in saying this can happen without punishment. With the rare child, that might be true (although I've never heard of this rare child), but it is not true of most children. If misbehavior does not cost the perpetrator, then the perpetrator has no reason to internalize anything other than the belief that he is free to misbehave.

When it comes to logical or natural consequences, Ginott gives examples such as serving a child a cold meal if he fails to come home on time for dinner, or not letting a child watch television until he's completed his homework. That's fine and dandy, and that sort of approach works very well with kids who are generally obedient, polite, and respectful. Those kids need only an occasional nudge. But forty years' worth of experience counseling parents tells me Ginott's approach is not going to work with kids who are downright defiant, belligerently disrespectful, and provocatively irresponsible. Those kids need a huge wake-up call, one that logical or natural consequences won't send.

Ginott never talks about how to deal with a child of that sort. He implies that big problems develop only when parents don't treat their kids with respect in the first place, when their responses to problem behaviors are punitive rather than educational, when they're impatient rather than tolerant. In other words, it's the parents' fault if a child has big problems of that nature. Reading his book, one comes away thinking that any child misbehavior can be handled effectively without punishment. That puts Faber's rant about me in perspective. When the bar is set at no punishment, then *any* punishment is extreme by comparison, and anyone who recommends any punishment at all, in any situation, is "hung up" on it.

Gordon Weighs In

Five years after Ginott published his book, Gordon published *Parent Effectiveness Training,* but it wasn't until after Gordon's book became popular that Ginott's book began attracting wide attention. Gordon's book bangs the antipunishment drum every bit as loudly as he bangs the antiauthority drum, contending that punishment causes psychological trauma:

Because punishment, by definition, often results in humiliation and deprivation of children, the ensuing frustration is bound to be damaging to their psychological and/or physical health.

This is a scare tactic, and by definition, scare tactics do not represent truth. As usual, Gordon makes a statement that he cannot, and does not, prove.

If parents who have punished their children realize the error of their ways after reading his book, Gordon not only recommends that they stop punishing, he also recommends they apologize to their kids for ever having punished and promise to never do it again:

Parents will want to communicate to the youngsters that punishment is not to be used anymore. . . . More is gained by an attitude of trust. . . . In the no-lose method, parents should simply assume that the kids will carry out the decision.

Actually, I agree. Parents should convey instructions and expectations to children such that positive expectation is conveyed. That's the problem with both threat and promise of reward—they convey negative expectation. In both cases, a parent is essentially saying, "I don't think you're going to comply." Expectation is a powerful force. In effect, it predicts the future. Telling a child that if he doesn't finish raking the yard by lunchtime you're going to punish him actually increases the likelihood that the yard won't be finished by lunchtime. But so does promising the child an ice cream lunch. Positive expectation is conveyed by simply saying, "You should have no problem finishing this by lunchtime."

But let's face it, conveying positive expectations doesn't always work. What then? All of the new parenting prophets conveniently avoided answering that question. They did so by claiming that if parents use their methods, blatant rebellion won't occur. It only occurs, they maintain, when parents don't follow their advice.

This causes me to question how much experience any of these folks had with flesh-and-blood children. I worked with children and families for nearly twenty years before I took up writing and speaking on a full-time basis. During those two decades, I ran across a good number of kids who seemed to have come out of the womb itching for a fight, determined to prove that no one could tell them what to do. In most cases, their siblings, both older and younger, were polite, obedient, happy kids. Their parents were good people who loved and wanted what was best for their children. Obviously, these parents had not caused the problem. I think Gordon, Ginott, and the other new parenting prophets blame the parents because they don't know what to do when confronted with children of this sort.

I say these kids need to pay a stiff penalty for their refusal to live according to civilized expectations. They don't need to be understood, and they certainly don't need to be given license to abuse and disrupt their families. Will punishment work? That's a good question. The fact is, some of these kids will eventually come around, and some won't. Nonetheless, they all need to pay the penalty. Sometimes, I am forced to ask parents, "Are you willing to accept that you are not the appointed agents concerning this issue in your child's life?" I long ago recognized that some kids are simply on a self-destructive trajectory that their parents are not going to alter, no matter what. In this very technological age, when no problem seems insurmountable, it's difficult to accept that certain problems with children can't be solved, but that's the way it sometimes is, I'm afraid.

I've said it in previous books, but it bears repeating: If a child does the wrong thing (over and over again), and his parents do the right thing (over and over again), there is no guarantee the child will stop doing the wrong thing. What works with dogs does not always work with human beings. But even when a child seems bent on self-destruction through defiance and disruption, his parents need to stay the course. They need to keep doing the right thing. They need to pray that someday he'll realize that he can't live according to his own rules and that there is a price to be paid for acting as such. Mind you, that's exactly the opposite of what Gordon and his coconspirators proposed. They proposed that children should be allowed to create and live by their own rules. That *their* feelings trumped everyone else's. This is postmodern relativism in its purest form. If taken to its logical conclusion, it results in social anarchy. And family anarchy is where social anarchy begins.

Gordon, Briggs, Ginott, and Faber were not simply wrong; they were dangerous. The implementation of their toxic ideas resulted in unhappier children, unhappier families, and contributed greatly to a much less healthy society.

Imagine No More Standards; It's Easy If You Try

Sociologists say we are now in the postmodern era, and one of postmodernity's defining characteristics is moral relativism, the notion that absolute standards of right and wrong are antiquated, an artifact of an earlier stage in the evolution of human intellect. Before her retirement, Oprah Winfrey occasionally used the term "your reality" when she was chatting with one of her guests. That's moral relativism at the level of the individual. Your reality may involve permission to commit adultery, at least under certain circumstances. Mine doesn't, under any circumstances. According to postmodernity, we're both entitled to our own opinions (another relativism). Wrong arises only when I assert that a person who commits adultery has done something wrong.

And so it is with Gordon, Briggs, and the others regarding children's behavior. Children don't do wrong things. They simply act out unresolved emotional conflicts and repressed feelings that are the result of uptight parents who try to make them do the "right" things, which are right only because of the parents' ingrained biases. In this thought system, there is no exceptional scenario that justifies a parent using punishment because *no child actually misbehaves.* Gordon says:

> *In our training programs we try to help parents see that children don't really misbehave . . . adults say a child misbehaves whenever some specific action is judged as contrary to how the adult* thinks *the child should behave. The verdict of misbehavior, then, is clearly a value judgment made by the adult. . . . The "badness" of the behavior actually resides in the adult's mind.*

That's an example of Gordon's chronically illogical thought processes. Consider: If child misbehavior is only in the eye of the beholder, then logic demands that adult misbehavior is also only in the eye of the beholder. Criminality is a value judgment made by noncriminals. To use Gordon's own argument, the "badness" of a crime is nothing more than a reflection of a cultural bias that has developed over time. The reader may think I'm being coy, but that exact thesis was the subject of a best-selling 1960s book. In *The Crime of Punishment* (Viking, 1966), well-known psychiatrist Karl Menninger concluded, "I suspect that all the crimes committed by all the jailed criminals do not equal in total social damage that of the crimes committed against them." In other words, just as Gordon and the others believed the misbehaving child is a victim, Menninger believed the adult criminal is a victim. And just as the self-esteemers believed punishing children is wrong, Menninger asserted that punishing adult criminals is wrong, a relic of an earlier, more brutal, less enlightened time in human history. As the self-esteemers believed about children, Menninger thought that adult criminals needed understanding. He believed recidivism could be prevented through psychiatric treatment (talking, understanding, giving the criminal a safe place within which to freely express his inner pain, and so on). To put the impact of Menninger's view in perspective, President Jimmy Carter awarded him the Medal of Freedom. Gordon was nominated for the Nobel Peace Prize. Menninger and Gordon have both been proven wrong, but their legacies live on, enshrined even.

Gordon contends that no child actually misbehaves, and if an adult thinks otherwise, there is something amiss with the adult. At the very least, the adult is in thrall to outdated concepts of right and wrong. So, a teenager who took his parents' brand new car without permission, used a fake ID to purchase beer, and drove around town under the influence of alcohol wasn't doing anything wrong. It was wrong only in his parents' narrow, unevolved minds. The child was only exercising his right to freedom of expression. Or the child was simply acting out his frustration at living with such backward, rigid, prejudiced, narrow-minded, unenlightened people. In either case, punishment is an inappropriate response. This teen car thief needs some understanding. When he reaches adulthood, he will become one of Menninger's patients.

In *Your Child's Self-Esteem*, Briggs gives the example of a mother whose toddler attempts to hit her while in the throes of one of his frequent tantrums. Briggs praises the mother for handing her child a pillow and encouraging him to demonstrate what he'd like to do to her for interrupting his play to make him go on an errand with her. As the child beats, throws, and rips the pillow, the mother encourages him with statements like, "Feels good to hurt that Mama!" and "You don't want to come with me, not at all!" According to Briggs, this mother is to be commended for helping her child express his feelings rather than falling into the self-esteem–endangering trap of disciplining (restraining, isolating) the toddler's tantrum. Instead, Briggs insists that this toddler will be much better off because he has been allowed to "keep his self-respect as a person who was no less worthy because of his violent reactions."

Imagine for a moment the sort of world this would be if people believed in "respecting" violent tantrums from adults. From this perspective, Briggs's advice is often utterly irrational. I'd even go so far as to say it's crazy.

Not to be outdone even by herself, Briggs goes on to celebrate a child's disrespect toward parents:

The child who openly expresses hostility to you actually hands you a double bouquet. You have reared him with enough strength to stand up for himself; he's no wilted violet. And you have made him feel safe to express himself directly. So if your child says "I don't like you," "You're mean," or "I wish I had someone else for a mother (father)," pat yourself on the back and stay with his feelings. He'll take you behind the code and then you can deal with the real issues—the primary emotions.

I propose that there's no value to either parent or child for a parent to "stay with" the child's feelings and try to "decode" the "real" problem in this sort of situation. The real problem is obvious: the child's belligerent disrespect. Parents should not pat themselves on the back for rearing a child who flaunts disdain for their authority; they should demonstrate their complete control of themselves and the situation. Perhaps some enforced contemplation in his room will cause the child to control his loose lips. An apology is certainly in order.

It's important for the reader to understand that the new parenting prophets were not out on the fringes. At the time, they were mainstream. Their point of view informed the teachings that psychology graduate students, including yours truly, were learning around that time. Most of my professors taught that a child's misbehavior is only a symptom of an unresolved emotional problem that lies deep within the child's subconscious mind. I learned that misbehavior was a child's way of "crying for help," a subconscious means of drawing attention to psychological distress caused by some family dysfunction caused, in turn, by parental tyranny or ignorance. The clinician's responsibility, therefore, is to gain the child's trust and then go beneath the surface to find and help resolve the psychological conflict that's causing the child to misbehave. In other words, a child who is disobedient, disrespectful, a bully, or irresponsible is not a responsible perpetrator; rather, he's a victim of adult-inflicted psychological damage that he is incapable of fixing. If this interpretation is true, then punishment will only compound the problem. Instead, the child needs a safe place where he can receive unconditional acceptance, permission to freely express his feelings and receive understanding, and sympathy. The bottom line: The child is not responsible for *anything* (literally) he does that is wrong by traditional standards.

This sort of unsound thinking is still alive and well in the mental health community. I was in a midwestern city a few years ago and came across a community magazine. In an advice column, a local and apparently respected therapist fielded a question from the parents of a four-year-old girl who threw frequent, wild tantrums whenever one of them—or any other authority figure, for that matter—failed to please her. Needless to say, the child consistently refused to comply with adult instructions and was disrespectful toward her parents and teachers. Furthermore, she had recently begun to bully other children at her preschool.

The therapist asserted that this little sociopath was simply expressing deep-seated psychological distress. She *needed* to misbehave in order to vent and resolve her inner frustrations. By extension, her parents were obviously doing something very wrong. Mind you, the therapist arrived at this conclusion based on no more information than I've given the reader. Instead of providing these parents with helpful guidance, she told them their child was in major psychic pain, pain *they* caused. As if disrespecting the parents wasn't enough, this "therapist" then told them the worst thing they could do was punish their daughter when she misbehaved. That would make her feel judged, send the message that her feelings were bad, and seriously damage her self-esteem, maybe irrevocably. They needed to love her even more, praise her liberally (for what?), talk to her, help her express her feelings in words, and generally act like they were seeking her forgiveness for the horrible things they'd done, whatever they were. This advice was nothing short of stupid. If the parents actually did what this incompetent "expert" told them to do, their little criminal was going to quickly turn into a little tyrant.

Over the years, hundreds of parents have told me that when they sought professional help for problems with their children, therapists took their children's side. Misbehaving, irresponsible children became victims, and the parents became villains. All too often, therapists magically transform children who need correction into injured parties who need sympathy and parents who need help into bad actors who need correction. In almost every one of these horror stories, the parents recall a therapist telling them their child was suffering from low self-esteem, the result, of course, of the parents' intolerance of disrespect, disobedience, lying, stealing, and other sociopathic traits. This is precisely why I tell parents that seeking professional help for problems with children is a risky thing to do. It is not that all mental health professionals are problem makers instead of problem solvers, it's that the risk of getting involved with a problem maker merits caution. In most other professions—medicine and law, for example—incompetent practitioners are eventually de-licensed. About the only thing a mental health professional can do to guarantee being stripped of professional privilege is have sexual relations with a client. Incompetence is not enough. In fact, as evidenced by the story I told in the Introduction, incompetent therapists are sometimes protected by their licensing authorities.

If the self-esteemers are correct, tantrums aren't antisocial outbursts that merit discipline; they are desperate messages from toddlers who are crying out for "constructive assistance." Acts of selfishness are not character flaws to be corrected; they are a natural part of establishing "separateness" that should be allowed unhindered in perpetuity. Rudeness is to be expected and tolerated from children. It may even be an indication that parents have succeeded at giving the rude child permission to express himself freely! Adults who insist that preteens be socially courteous are expecting too much and "devaluing the child" in the process. A child who steals is trying to fill a psychological "hole" by stuffing it with other people's belongings. A child who lies is expressing fear of unrealistic parental expectations. Misbehavior, no matter the form, is a psychological code that demands encryption. And it's all the fault of authority-mongering parents. Children are innocents. The unceasing babble is mind-numbing.

Bad Is a Bad Word

This point of view—that children are fundamentally good—is belied by the fact that one does not have to teach a child bad behavior. A child enters the world carrying a bagful of bad. Shortly after he begins to talk, he begins to lie. Mind you, he lies in the absence of anyone lying to or in front of him. Without any like examples from role models in their lives, toddlers hit their parents, steal, defy, shout nasty things at the very people who love them the most, and bully other children in order to get what those other children have.

Curing a child's inborn antisocial nature requires lots of unconditional love and lots of forceful discipline. Without the balancing effect of discipline, love becomes distorted and expresses itself as enabling. Without the balancing effect of love, discipline becomes distorted and expresses itself as abuse. The forceful discipline in question does not need to be physical (although there are times with certain children when forceful spankings are appropriate); it simply needs to be full of loving force, an unwavering determination on the part of the child's parents to raise a responsible citizen.

The reader surely noticed that I included stealing in the litany of inborn misbehavior. Hearing that, someone once reprovingly told me, "Toddlers don't know they're stealing."

My response: "Then why do they hide what they take, and why, when they are confronted, do they deny they have taken it?"

By his or her second birthday, perhaps even before, an intelligent human being has intuited the concept of possession and wants what other people have. More specifically, he wants things they take pleasure and pride in. He wants other children's favorite toys. He wants his sibling's favorite shoes. He wants his mother's pearl necklace. He covets, but he does not covet ordinary things like plastic spoons. He covets the very things that other people value. He's a natural-born thief, not a natural-born respecter of other people's property.

Toddlers believe that what they want they deserve to have. And because they deserve what they want, the end justifies the means. Anyone who's lived with a toddler has seen dramatic, often violent demonstrations of this belief system. Adult criminals possess the same mentality. The "natural" child, therefore, is an antisocial narcissist. In two previous books, I refer to the toddler as the "Little Criminal." If a child's natural inclinations are not properly exorcised, the child is likely to grow up into a sociopath. That's why love and understanding are not enough.

The self-esteemers understood none of this. They began from a false premise: The child was by nature good, pure, unsullied. Their mission was the preservation of the child's natural goodness. Therefore, they reasoned, love and understanding were enough.

Children have great difficulty accepting responsibility for their misdeeds. This is one of the hurdles separating the valid adult from the perpetual child, the men from the boys. Responsibility must be *forced* on children. Not beaten into them, mind you—*forced* upon them by parents and teachers who stay on a determined course in the kids' lives. The force in question demands punishment for misdeeds. When this force is lacking, it is difficult for a child to grow up. In light of the dramatic rise in the age of successful emancipation since 1970, it would indeed appear that children are having a very difficult time growing up. I propose that this difficulty is largely the inevitable result of the therapeutic parenting and educational culture that has arisen since then.

Don't Get Hung Up

Punishment is not always the answer to a problem behavior, mind you. Different kids demand different solutions, and there really isn't one formula. I told the parents of a six-year-old girl who was throwing frequent, full-bore tantrums to tell her they'd spoken to a doctor who said that tantrums at age six meant she wasn't getting enough sleep. To help Little Miss Fit stop tantruming, the doctor prescribed a 6:30 bedtime, two hours before her regular bedtime. When the tantrums had stopped for a month—meaning she had caught up on all of her lost sleep—her regular bedtime would be restored. The tantrums stopped almost immediately.

Note that the consequence, although clearly "punitive," was not presented as such. In effect, it was a punishment placebo. The problem was also redefined. The little girl's tantrums were transformed from misbehavior into a symptom of chronic lack of sufficient sleep. Finally, the authority in the situation was shifted to a third party, one whose authority the child already respected. One tantrum-free month later, regular bedtime was restored and the child's tantrums were never repeated. And the little girl was much happier for it.

But what if she had rebelled against early bedtime? What if she had refused to go to bed? I was fairly certain the doctor's prescription would work because tantrums were the only problem. Otherwise, she was polite, reasonably obedient, and well liked by other adults and children. Why were the tantrums occurring in the first place? I had no idea, and I didn't really care. I speculated that the parents had never fully cured the terrible twos, and the girl's ongoing tantrums were just a bad habit with four years of momentum behind it. If my theory was correct, then no one was at fault. The child wasn't "bad," and neither were the parents. The important thing was that the tantrums stopped and all ended well.

What would Gordon, Briggs, Faber, or Ginott have recommended in that situation? I don't have a clue, other than to say with confidence that none of them would not have recommended what the doctor ordered. My point is that punishment is not the answer for everything, but it is decidedly unhelpful if a mental health professional tells parents that it's not the answer to *anything*.

Take an eight-year-old boy who was defiant and disrespectful toward his parents. He wouldn't do *anything* they told him to do. One day he came home from school to a room that was completely stripped of all of possessions except essential clothing. His parents had taken everything he "owned"—toys, favorite clothes, collections—to a storage facility. They told him he would have to live that way until he decided to be 100 percent obedient and respectful toward them.

The parents put a chart with thirty blocks on the refrigerator. When he had a "perfect" day—no disobedience, no talking back—he could put a star in one of the blocks at the end of the day, right before bedtime. He received no reward for a good day other than the satisfaction of being able to "star" himself. When he had managed thirty perfect days in a row, he would get his favorite things back. One act of defiance or disrespect constituted a bad day; he would be sent to his room for its duration. In that event, the old chart was taken down and a new one was put up. He had seven bad days before having one perfect day. (Let me be perfectly clear; being obedient and respectful is not asking too much of an eight-year-old child, nor is asking for thirty days of obedience and respect.) Then he managed five perfect days in a row, then eight, then fifteen, then thirty. Voilà! His parents restored his room, and that was that. The problem was cured in sixty-five days. And the cure involved no therapy, testing, diagnosis, or drugs. But it did involve punishment. This little fellow needed a huge wake-up call. I saw the mother a year later. She told me her son was a much, much happier child. Of course! People who obey legitimate authority figures are much happier than people who don't. That applies to adults as well as children, by the way.

That sixty-five-day cure is most definitely not the sort of thing Faber, Ginott, Gordon, or Briggs would approve of. They would claim that an approach of that sort would violate the boy's need to have his parents understand his feelings. It would cause him to feel that his feelings were bad, and therefore so was he. It would deny him needed autonomy, make him feel worthless, cause guilt, and so on. Horsefeathers! That punitive approach caused the child to make the decision he needed to make: He was going to obey and respect his parents. That decision was good for his parents, but it was even better for him. Someone could have talked himself blue in the face trying to understand the boy's misbehavior, and he would not have made that decision. He made it because he was *forced* to make it. Unfortunately, sometimes benign force is the only answer to a behavior problem.

Sometimes when I describe an approach of that sort, someone will accuse me of being harsh. What is harsh about it? The child's room, even devoid of favorite things, was a comfortable place. It was heated in the winter and cooled in the summer. It was clean and vermin free. The bed was cozy. The room had a window that looked out on trees and grass and bushes and other green things. When that little boy was confined to his room, he was bored, that's all. To impose boredom on someone for a short period of time is not harsh. Let's be real: During those sixty-five days, that little boy lived in better conditions than most of the world's children. When the sixty-five days were up, he was no less healthy than when they had started. He had lost no weight, he had not become ill, he was not catatonic. During the punishment period, he was fed, clothed, and treated with love. He is not deserving of any pity.

Again, punishment is not the only answer to all behavior problems, but sometimes it's the only possible answer to a specific behavior problem. Gordon, Briggs, Faber, and Ginott failed to see that. They denied parents permission to use a disciplinary tool that should not be used often but would have to be used sometimes, and more often than sometimes with certain kids. In so doing, they created more problems for parents than they solved. And as parenting goes, so goes America.

Toilet Babble

"Babble, babble, toilet trouble."

—THE THREE GRANDMOTHERS IN
JOHN ROSEMOND'S ADAPTATION OF *MACBETH*

No single child-rearing task has been more adversely affected by parent-babble than toilet training. Herein lies the tale of how experts—and one in particular—turned a simple teaching process into a confusing quasi-science, made a mountain out of a molehill, and contributed greatly to the stress women associate with child rearing.

Before the 1960s, it was rare to find a child older than twenty-four months who was not using the toilet reliably and successfully. In the mid-1950s, for example, research conducted by social scientists at several major universities, including Harvard and Stanford, found that more than 80 percent of American children had been successfully toilet trained—defined as accident free for one month—by twenty-four months.

There is no indication whatsoever that the pre-1960s mom thought toilet training was a big deal, much less a potentially apocalyptic psychological event that might, if mishandled, scar her child's psyche. I've asked women who toilet trained their kids by twenty-four months in the 1950s and 1960s how they went about it. They consistently say they dispensed with diapers, showed their children the potty seat, helped them onto it when necessary, made it clear they were no longer permitted to "wee-wee" or "stinky" in their clothing, and helped them clean up when they were done. When their children had accidents, the women responded without anger, firmly reminding the children what they should do. In short, the moms approached this hurdle straightforwardly, matter-of-factly, calmly, and authoritatively. Most important, they made their expectations perfectly clear, which is 90 percent of successful discipline no matter the issue. Almost all of these moms, now great- and even great-great-grandmothers, report that the entire process took less than a week, two weeks at most. They do not remember toilet training being associated with stress of any sort. They don't remember their kids resisting, holding, or hiding, things all too many of today's moms deal with.

Today, the child who is fully trained by twenty-four months is the exception, and most American children don't become accident free until after their third birthdays. Holding, hiding, refusing, having deliberate "accidents," tantrums over using the toilet—all have become common. For today's mom, toilet training is probably the single most stressful undertaking of the preschool years. She dreads it. She worries that she's not interpreting her child's readiness signs properly. She worries she's going to do it in a manner that damages her child's delicate psyche, causes him to have "toileting issues," or results in feelings of confusion toward his own bodily wastes. She approaches training hesitantly, with great anxiety, and fails to communicate authority or clear expectations. When her child has an accident, she tells him not to worry, it's okay, and then turns around and becomes upset when he has another accident. When her child is finally trained at three-and-one-half, she reports that it took from six months to over a year.

The biology of children has not changed since the 1950s. The human bladder and bowels have not become weaker, nor does it take longer for them to develop, thus predisposing children to significantly longer periods of training. So what is going on here? How is it that something a 1950s mom did in a week or two with a child who had not yet reached his second birthday is now taking months, even years, and rarely produces an accident-free child before age three?

The problem is experts, and one in particular: pediatrician T. Berry Brazelton. But in order to put Brazelton's mischief in proper perspective, we have to turn back the clock more than one hundred years, to the man who was Brazelton's primary inspiration.

Freud or Fraud?

Sigmund Freud, the so-called father of modern psychology, was the first expert to weigh in on toilet training, and it is accurate to say that concerning the mental health profession's proclivity for psychobabble, Freud takes the prize for Greatest Psychobabbler of All Time. Those who came after him are mere wannabes, however much damage they have caused.

Freud believed that during the preschool years (birth through five), a child's psychological development is shaped by oral, anal, and Oedipal "psychosexual" stages. Each stage is defined by a critical event, and if it is not handled properly by the child's parents, it will cause grave psychological problems later in life.

During the anal phase—between a child's first and third birthdays, approximately—the critical event is toilet training. Freud hypothesized that if toilet training were done too early, too late, or punitively, the child's personality would become "fixated" at that stage of development, resulting in an "anal" personality characterized by compulsive neatness, stinginess, and stubbornness. In his 1908 essay "Character and Anal Eroticism," Freud also posited that fixation at the anal stage could explain homosexuality, paranoia, chronic constipation, and a preoccupation with money. It's important to note that Freud did not arrive at his conclusions by using any process that even approximates the scientific method. He did nothing but talk with his patients, and from those conversations he drew conclusions that he then generalized to everyone. In other words, Freud pulled his theories out of thin air, but he did not regard them as theories. According to some of his contemporaries, Freud believed he was incapable of being wrong about anything.

The fact is that none of his theories have stood up under objective scientific investigation. For example, no correlation has been found between adult personality characteristics and toilet training. But Freud's far-fetched ideas continue to influence a good number of psychiatrists and psychologists to this day. As we shall soon see, his nonsense also exerted significant influence on the advice dispensed by the very well-intentioned architect of America's toilet-training woes.

Pediatrician Benjamin Spock was the next expert to have significant influence on toilet training. In his 1946 classic, *The Common-Sense Book of Baby and Child Care,* Spock told mothers they could begin training as soon as a baby could sit up on his own (well before the first birthday), but he also said it was perfectly all right to start later. He said that regardless of when a mom decided to start training, the most important elements were her attitude and approach *during the child's second year of life.* Spock preached patience and understanding while recommending that mothers approach training with a "casual and friendly" attitude. Good advice, overall. But then, with one afterthought, Spock kicked off the wrongheaded notion that if left to his own devices, a child would train himself on schedule: "If you want to be completely natural, you can leave bowel training almost entirely up to your baby . . . [who] will probably take himself to the toilet before he is two [years old]."

Spock's intention was to help mothers approach toilet training with a relaxed attitude, which was good considering the rigid approach many professionals had previously recommended. Unfortunately, he also gave permission to mothers to leave training almost completely up to their children. He probably had no idea that others would take his aside concerning self-training and ultimately extend it to justify the wearing of diapers by children age three and older. Clearly, Spock believed children should be trained by their second birthdays.

From the early 1950s on, the notion that "readiness" played a part in successful toilet training steadily grew. In his 1968 revision of *Baby and Child Care*, Spock—whose overall parenting philosophy had moved in a liberal, permissive direction over the previous twenty-two years—had come up with five readiness signs for bowel training:

◆ The child is proud of his bowel movements.

◆ He begins to take joy in giving things to others.

◆ His mother's approval is important to him.

◆ He is fascinated with putting things in containers.

◆ He warns of an impending bowel movement.

Unfortunately, by introducing a list of readiness indicators, Spock began to soil the waters of toilet training, and the matter of readiness became more and more confusing. It is interesting that Spock rightly observes that using or not using diapers is a strong statement by itself, and he recommends the latter:

To continue to put diapers on a child who is gaining control is an expression of lack of confidence. A diaper invites wetting and soiling.

I couldn't agree more. In fact, having the child run naked during training is central to my "Naked and $75" method, which I fully explained in *Toilet Training Without Tantrums* (Andrews McMeel, 2012). The method is a slightly Westernized version of the very simple, straightforward approach used by mothers worldwide for hundreds if not thousands of years and still widely used in many developing cultures.

Interestingly, Spock also recognized that parents who tend to be avid consumers of parent education materials may be putting themselves at a distinct disadvantage. He noted that in one of the clinics in the medical school in which he taught, the parents who had the greatest success with toilet training were those without college degrees or interest in psychology. He observed that their children tended to be trained before their second birthdays, without struggle or harm to their personalities. Along the same lines, I've made numerous public statements to the effect that parents who think and read too much tend to create unnecessary problems for themselves and their children (that cringe you hear is coming from my publisher).

Spock did not intend that his five readiness indicators would be anything more than general markers for parents who needed more than intuition to know when to start training. He had no idea that the next significant potty pundit, whose star was already ascending in 1968, would eventually extend readiness to mean that a parent should do exactly what Spock recommended against: stop at every sign of resistance and put the child back in diapers.

T. Berry Brazelton and Child-Centered Toilet Training

In 1962, the influential medical journal *Pediatrics* published "A Child-Oriented Approach to Toilet Training," by T. Berry Brazelton. In it, Brazelton summarized what is properly called field research he had carried out in his Cambridge, Massachusetts pediatric clinic between 1951 and 1961. In this influential article, Brazelton took the position that toilet training should be postponed until after the second birthday, his premise being that the pre-two child's nervous system was not sufficiently mature and that a child's interest in bladder and bowel control would increase during his third year of life, as did his general desire for independence and mastery.

Brazelton's article became the springboard for his ever-expanding notions about readiness. He likened toilet training to learning to walk. When a child's nervous system and muscle control have matured to a certain level, a child will walk. No one has to *teach* him to walk. All parents have to do is provide the opportunity (uncluttered space and sturdy objects the child can use to pull himself to a standing position), and walking will begin around a child's first birthday. Brazelton also proposed that when a child's nervous system and muscle control mature to a certain level, the child will begin controlling his bowels and bladder, and with minimal guidance, he will start to use the toilet. No one would have to *make* him use the toilet. He would use the toilet *because he wants to,* just as he wants to walk, talk, and master other skills.

Brazelton was comparing apples to watermelons. Walking comes naturally to a child; it is programmed into the development of the nervous system. Relieving bodily waste in a toilet, on the other hand, is not "natural" at all. Natural is squatting down and relieving oneself whenever and wherever the urge strikes. And as many of today's moms will attest, a child left to his own devices will be content to relieve himself *naturally* in his diapers indefinitely.

It would be more apt to compare learning to use the toilet with learning to eat with utensils rather than one's hands (the *natural* way to eat). As is the case with using the toilet, a child will eat with his hands until his parents show him how to use utensils. Both are skills that are necessary to living in civilized social groups, and both must be taught. Brazelton began with a false premise, but no one questioned it. His ideas were new, and because this was the 1960s, they gained immediate traction in the medical community. Brazelton became America's resident potty pundit, and toilet training would never be the same.

Virtually overnight, pediatricians began encouraging parents to let their children train themselves, noting Brazelton's use of the term "child-oriented" in his article's title. This overnight change in belief is an example of what two researchers observed in a 1977 analysis of toilet training trends: "Infant care writers (tend to change) opinions in unison, without the benefit of strong empirical evidence."

Since publication of that 1962 article, Brazelton has not conducted any research that would qualify as truly scientific. He has only collected anecdotal reports from parents, who are not the most objective reporters when it comes to behavior of their own children.

Nonetheless, he claims to have conclusively identified toilet training's readiness signs. He states that pre-two training—because at that age the child is rarely ready, according to Brazelton's unscientific criteria—is potentially harmful and requires excessive parental pressure, and he assures parents that it is not at all problematic for intelligent human beings to continue soiling and wetting themselves until they are three or even four years old. Those are my words, not Brazelton's, but it is a fair characterization of his message.

Freud Redux

Over the years, Brazelton has been fond of using dramatic, conjectural statements to support his contentions. Here are two such examples from his 1974 book *Toddlers and Parents:*

◆ He asserts that children "value the bowel movement as part of themselves and worry about it going down the drain."

◆ After watching young children play with a large toilet display at a children's museum, he concludes that children need to work through a certain amount of anxiety over using the toilet.

These are prime examples of toilet babble. Like Freud (and Gordon, Briggs, Faber, and Ginott), Brazelton dispenses far-fetched notions that are not rooted in the intellectually rigorous process of scientific inquiry. In short, like Freud, he's making this stuff up.

One must wonder how Brazelton came to know that toddlers attach "value" to their bowel movements and experience anxiety at seeing them flushed away. Did he ask a focus group of toddlers, "Do you feel a sense of attachment concerning your poopy? Does flushing it down the toilet cause you to feel unsettled?" No, he did not.

In fact, toddlers are generally awestruck by flushing and will want to do it over and over again. That's why they are likely, when their parents aren't looking, to put all manner of objects into the toilet and try to flush them away. Toddlers are a plumber's best friends. For the typical toddler, flushing is not anxiety arousing. It's sport! They are also fascinated with the play possibilities inherent in poop, as they are interested in the play possibilities of everything else. That's why, if left to their own devices, many of them discover the joys of finger painting with their poop. The desire to explore and experiment is the dominant characteristic of toddlerhood, not anxiety over where things go when they are flushed down the toilet.

However, Brazelton is not alone in this fanciful notion that flushing causes young children to feel ill at ease. On his Web site, pediatrician and author William Sears (whose attachment parenting theories take up another chapter in this book) claims that many children "are afraid of seeing parts of themselves come out of their body and go swoosh down the drain." Really? I am not aware of any objective evidence that supports this imaginative contention. It is pure, unmitigated poppycock or, I should say, *poopy*cock.

Trying to prove the point, Brazelton goes on to say that toddlers become worried about where bathtub water goes when it drains out of the tub, and he further stretches credulity by asserting that toddlers worry "whether they might get sucked down too." Excuse me? I've worked with parents and children for forty years, and I helped raise two children to whom I gave numerous baths when they were toddlers. My kids thought activating the drain was entertaining and wanted to remain in the tub until all the water was gone. That is the norm, not children jumping up and beginning to scream when the drain is activated. Because anything is possible, I'll grant that some child, somewhere, has developed this fear, but to suggest that it is common is indefensible. Brazelton even claims that some children may worry about something coming back up the bathtub drain or the toilet bowl. It sounds as if he's read one too many Stephen King novels.

Concerning the idea that kids playing with an oversize toilet are trying to work through related psychological anxieties, let me assure the reader that children taking such delight is no more psychologically significant than children enjoying play with toy kitchens. Intelligent people would scoff at the idea that when children play in toy kitchens they are actually trying to work through a certain amount of "food preparation anxiety," yet when Brazelton proposes essentially the same absurdity concerning children playing with an oversized toilet, intelligent people, even physicians, believe him.

These two examples make it obvious that Brazelton has been greatly influenced by Freudian theory. It's understandable, given that he did postgraduate study in child psychiatry at Massachusetts General Hospital in the 1950s, when Freud's influence in academia, and especially psychiatry, was at its peak. In fact, it often sounds like he's channeling Freud. It's interesting to note that Freud's contemporary, psychiatrist Hans Eysenck, compared him to the brothers Grimm and other creators of children's fantasy. Similarly, Brazelton's speculations on the inner workings of the young child's psyche are highly imaginative.

Brazelton's fantastical speculations know no bounds. On the matter of changing diapers, he proposes that when a child gives up diapers he gives up a certain amount of intimacy that parents must make up for in other ways. He asks, "Why would a two-year-old want to give up these close times for a cold potty?" Here he raises the notion that toilet training disrupts the parent–child bond. To today's mother, inundated by attachment babble (the subject of an upcoming chapter), few things are more anxiety arousing than the notion she isn't properly bonding with her child. Brazelton warns against traumatizing children but seems to have no problem traumatizing mothers. In fact, largely because of this sort of fantastical toilet babble, toilet training for many if not most mothers has become stressful, anxiety arousing, frustrating, and guilt ridden. For some, it proves to be the most negative experience of their entire motherhoods, and no wonder. After all, Brazelton basically tells parents that in order to toilet train properly, they must become quasi-therapists to their children so as to prevent or minimize the potential psychological damage.

In all fairness, Brazelton constantly emphasizes what is undeniably true: Ultimately, the child will decide whether and when to use the toilet. Pressuring a child to use the toilet will almost surely backfire. Brazelton makes his mistake in equating *any* initiative on a parent's part with pressure. But when all is said and done, the parent will have to initiate toilet training because even when the window of maximum opportunity is most open—between eighteen and twenty-four months—only the rare child will initiate the process himself, much less self-train.

Let's face it: Toilet training—like teaching any other social skill, including table manners, proper greetings, and so on—is a parental responsibility. I've never heard of a child developing proper table manners on his own, without parental correction and teaching. Make no mistake about it: Learning to dispose of one's own body wastes discreetly and properly is a social skill that is necessary to civilizing a human being. It is one of many learned behaviors that distinguishes us from beasts and enables us to live cooperatively in organized social groups. The child who does not master this skill is going to offend people, just as he would if he sat at someone's table and ate like a hyena. Furthermore, the earlier a child benefits from this civilizing influence, the better for everyone.

Readiness, Schmediness

In his 1992 book *Touchpoints,* Brazelton shrugs off any toileting interest on the part of pre–two-year-olds. To a mother who comments that her pre-two child is aware of his bowel movements and pulls at his diaper, Brazelton responds that this only means, "When the time comes, he will want to be in control of his own toilet habits." Wrong. It means he finds a messy diaper uncomfortable. I would tell this mother that the time has come to help her child learn what he is obviously capable of learning and will want to learn as soon as he realizes the pleasures of dry, clean clothing. That Brazelton actually discouraged this mother from toilet training a child who is capable of mastering the task is beyond wrongheaded. Unfortunately, it is his tendency.

Several years ago, I received an e-mail from the mother of a child who had shown desire to use the toilet before twelve months and had mastered the process in no time. The mother told me she called Brazelton to ask whether he'd ever heard of this in a child so young. She said that Brazelton became upset and accused her of "forcing" her infant to use the toilet, implying that she had already done the child great harm. In this regard, evidence abounds that until the 1940s, many children in America were using the toilet successfully before their first birthdays, and there is no evidence that such early toilet training caused psychological harm to those kids, and almost all of those kids, according to Brazelton's definition of the term, were forced. To this mother's credit, she stood her ground and told Brazelton she really wasn't interested in his editorial comments; she only wanted to know whether he'd heard of this before. For him to deny the obvious—that the child was obviously ready to use the toilet before she turned one and that toilet training her had been a cakewalk—means that Brazelton doesn't want to hear anything that might contradict his personal belief system.

In *Touchpoints,* Brazelton warns parents against starting toilet training before his five signs of supposed readiness are exhibited. That means the child:

◆ Is over the excitement of walking and likes to sit down.

◆ Understands simple distinctions, such as the difference between the parents' toilet and his potty.

◆ Likes to imitate others, especially his parents.

◆ Possesses an appreciation for orderliness (e.g., he puts things in their proper place), "which can be transferred to urine and bowel movements."

◆ Isn't negative when given instructions.

These five indicators create the impression that Brazelton has delved deeply into the mysteries of toilet training. They put a pseudoscientific aura around a process that is not complex and is hardly scientific. It's also significant and highly ironic that Brazelton's five readiness signs are present in many an eighteen-month-old child. Yet in virtually the next breath he warns against toilet training a child that age.

Keep in mind that in the mid-1950s, when researchers from several major universities found that more than 80 percent of American children were successfully trained by age twenty-four months, close to 100 percent of America's parents paid no heed to readiness signs, and there's no evidence that this ubiquitous ignorance resulted in any harm to children. Personally, I have yet to encounter a member of my generation who has had debilitating psychological blockages when it comes to eliminating body waste or being in the presence of white porcelain objects.

After providing a useless if not confounding set of supposed readiness criteria, Brazelton describes the steps necessary to successful toilet training, always reminding parents they should allow a child to refuse to use the toilet and immediately put him back in diapers after an accident so as not to make him "feel like a failure." How he knows that a toddler who has just had an accident and whose parents do not return him to diapers will feel like a failure is yet another mystery. In fact, this is an example of Brazelton's habit of making unsupportable claims that mystify an uncomplicated process, thus increasing the potential for parent anxiety. Concerning diapers and accidents, I contend (consistent with Spock) that once the decision is made to toilet train a child, nothing short of a major illness necessitating the child's hospitalization or some other prolonged emergency (more than a brief bump in the road, in other words) is sufficient cause for calling off the training. Nothing will kill the success or ease of toilet training more effectively than starting, then stopping and returning the child to diapers, then waiting, then starting, then stopping, and so on.

On the matter of accidents, most experts advise that when a child in training has one, the parents should reassure him that it's okay. Rubbish. It's *not* okay, and the child should most definitely not hear a message that contradicts what his parents expect him to do. There's a way of doing that without telling the child he's a miserable failure: "You pooped/wee-weed on yourself. When you feel a poop/wee-wee coming, you must sit down on your potty like I showed you, and put your poop/wee-wee in there. I know you can do it, and you'll do better next time." A message of that sort gives accurate feedback, restates the parent's expectation, reinforces the goal, and sends an empowering message to the child: "I know you can and will do this."

Brazelton would probably disapprove, and even some readers might be taken aback at the tone of that straightforward statement. Some might even feel it's a bit negative. The fact is, the statement is truthful, and even very young children can tolerate the truth when it's plainly and noncritically spoken. The child has just made a mistake. In order for him to improve his performance and eventually master this new task, it is vital that he receive accurate feedback and clear, supportive instructions from his parents. It's one thing to calmly say, "You had an accident, and you didn't do what I told you to do"; it's quite another to yell, "You're a miserable brat!" at the top of your lungs. In short, it is possible to tell a child he's made a mistake without making him feel worthless.

At the core of Brazelton's toilet training approach is the belief that using the toilet is just too much to ask of a pre–two-year-old. He tirelessly reminds parents that the requirements of toilet training result in enormous and sometimes incapacitating pressures on children. He seems to feel it's a shame that we have to expect this of them at all. According to Brazelton, any refusal, show of anxiety, hesitation, or unusual behavior on the part of the child is because toilet training involves so much psychological stress. In recognition of the harm that this enormously demanding and potentially traumatic process can force on a child, he says parents should immediately back off and revert to diapers if the child has an accident: "Repeated failures are likely to occur because [the child is] just not ready. Diapers need to be used . . . as a way of relieving her from the fear of making mistakes." Hear me clearly: This is very bad advice.

Remember, *accidents are inevitable*. Parents who follow Brazelton's advice to a T will wind up starting and stopping the process numerous times, thus giving the child no clear and consistent message as to their expectations. *That's* confusing.

In the final analysis, and for all his claims of respecting children, Brazelton seriously underestimates their capabilities. He may want to do nothing more than make parenting easier and more enjoyable, but he causes parents to have great anxiety and to question the legitimacy of their own authority.

By 2004, Brazelton had expanded his five readiness signs to seven. Quite frankly, they aren't worth listing. It is sufficient to note that, once again, he cloaks what is essentially a contrivance in the guise of science. Then he indulges in even more toilet babble. A two-year-old, he says, has developed a sense of what child development specialists call object permanence. This refers to the understanding that objects continue to exist even when they are removed from sight. Brazelton says this ability is a prerequisite of the child being "ready to say goodbye to poop." No kidding.

Statements of this sort cause me to question whether Brazelton is as well versed in the field of child development as most people— including pediatricians and child psychologists—seem to think. In the first place, it has long been known in child development circles that object permanence, first identified by Swiss psychologist Jean Piaget, is fairly well established by eight or nine months of age. In recent years, several researchers have even challenged that, saying it is established even earlier.

In the second place, although I happen to think that it's great and foolish fun for parent and child to stand over the toilet while the flush is swirling and say, "Bye-bye poop!" I think it's downright silly to imply that this is somehow essential to the child's mental health, that it helps him deal with potentially overpowering feelings of loss and separation.

Brazelton goes on to say that imitation becomes "more exciting and complex" shortly after a child turns two and that two-year-olds imitate one another during play. Neither of these statements is consistent with established developmental knowledge.

First, imitation of adults, especially parents, can be an indicator of a child's willingness to cooperate with those same adults. That does not describe two-year-olds. Twos have a reputation for being "terrible" for good reasons. Imitation usually peaks between the third and fourth birthdays.

Second, two-year-olds most definitely do *not* tend to imitate one another during play. Even in a group setting, the typical two-year-old child's play is solitary. He doesn't pay much attention to what other kids are doing until he notices what one of them is playing with, at which point he's likely to try and snatch it. In a group setting, two-year-olds are like separate island nations that launch occasional preemptive strikes at one another.

Brazelton further claims that toilet training will be easier after the second birthday because two-year-olds want to please their parents. That certainly does not describe most of the twos I've known or encountered vicariously through parental description. Most of those toddlers have been notably displeasing to one vexing degree or another. The typical toddler does not want to please; rather, he wants to be pleased. He does not want to obey; he wants to be obeyed. One wonders whether Brazelton really and truly knows children or only has preconceived ideas about them.

Readiness propaganda is prevalent in both modern parenting resources and the mainstream media. Take parenting pundit Elizabeth Pantley, for example. In *The No-Cry Potty Training Solution,* published in 2006, Pantley recommends that potty training take place during the "magical age span" of two-and-one-half to four. Remember that research has determined that the risk of problems increases significantly after Pantley's recommended—"magical"—start time of thirty months. In her book, she supports training from what she calls the "more common toddler-readiness approach."

Indeed, the pseudoscientific readiness approach is the more common approach these days, but to cite one example among many, it's also common for today's parents to allow pacifiers well past the second birthday, long past the time experts advise that their use be discontinued. In other words, the fact that a parenting practice is common is no recommendation. But given the fact that the professional community has rallied around the notion of toilet readiness, it's no wonder it has captivated so many American parents, who now tend to be skeptical of any notions that run counter to it. "Early" toilet training once meant twelve to eighteen months, but now its popular meaning is that age thirty months is the earliest a child will be ready, with most children being ready around age three. Most contemporary toilet babblers say it is not a problem if a child shows lack of readiness until age four or even older. So now we have what I call "Little Depends": disposable diapers that fit children up to fifty pounds and forty-two inches tall, which are averages for children ages four through six.

To the disgrace of the profession, many pediatricians have a blanket policy of discouraging parents from beginning to train until age three at the earliest. These pediatricians often assure parents their children will train themselves without much assistance sometime between ages three and four. This wrongheaded advice, taken straight from Brazelton's playbook, has caused parents tremendous grief, especially when they find themselves dealing with a four-year-old who not only shows no interest in using the toilet but absolutely refuses to sit on it, no matter what enticements his parents present. What parents hear from their pediatricians and the media is further reinforced in many a parent peer group, where it is heretical for a mother to violate the group's implied understanding that no child will be trained before age three. I have heard numerous testimonies from mothers who suddenly became persona non grata among their friends simply because they dared to violate this norm and toilet train their children "early."

Even parents who have little if any toilet training anxieties have been led to believe that if they wait until their children are at least three before toilet training, it will be a breeze. So they wait, and the convenience of disposable diapers means that they pay no significant price (other than the unnecessary cost of the disposables themselves) during the waiting. They pay a heavy emotional price later, when they decide they've waited long enough and try to persuade their kids to give sitting on the toilet a try. But who can blame them? The typical parent has no way of knowing that the concept of readiness was invented, cut from whole cloth. The average parent has no way of knowing that not one of the following claims is supported by credible scientific evidence:

◆ Certain specific developmental milestones must be cleared before successful toilet training can begin (historical evidence does not support this).

◆ The older the child, the easier toilet training will be (exactly the opposite is true, as we will see).

◆ Toilet training a child before supposed readiness behaviors emerge will harm the child's psychological development (unsupported by any objectively gathered evidence).

"But what about self-training?" a reader asks. "If a parent does wait, will the child eventually train himself?"

I have heard very few stories of children who, on their own and without the slightest hint from their parents, spontaneously signaled they wanted to use the potty and used it without incident from that point. They roughly equal the number of children I know of who learned to read on their own before going to school. And almost every story of self-training has involved a child who was not yet two years old. In fact, the "Naked and $75" method I present in *Toilet Training Without Tantrums* is a guided self-training model. I am convinced that the less involved parents are in the process, the more quickly children master the skill. In the context of my very old-fashioned model, the parent is a consultant who merely sets the stage properly, communicates properly, and responds to mistakes properly. I trust that the child does indeed want mastery, but unlike Brazelton, I am convinced that the optimal time to introduce this opportunity for mastery is before age two.

Once Again, the Child Rules

Brazelton simply does not acknowledge—one might go so far as to say he denies—the importance of the parent's role in toilet training. His advice is childcentric to a fault. He believes that the child's feelings should dominate any other consideration. For example, if the child balks at using the toilet, the parent should put diapers back on him. If he has an accident, the parent should put diapers back on him. If he displays any anxiety over sitting on the toilet and releasing, the parent should back off and put diapers back on him. This is the sort of advice that drives mothers to crazed confusion.

Brazelton's advice arises from his belief that toilet training is fraught with apocalyptic psychological consequences. By communicating this belief to parents, he causes them to dread toilet training, to approach it with trepidation and anxiety, and to send children mixed messages about exactly what is expected. A child who senses that his parents are not sure of themselves—and young children sense this intuitively—will respond by resisting his parents' tense efforts to move him toward sitting and releasing on the toilet.

Toilet training, like any other teaching, requires a show of calm, purposeful authority, an authority that communicates to the child exactly what he should do; an authority that is not afraid to speak correctively to the child when correction is called for. For a child to become convinced that he can master using the toilet, his parents must have complete confidence in his ability to do it. Brazelton's advice weakens parental confidence, weakens parental resolve, and sets the stage for unnecessary toilet training hassles.

Please understand me on this point: The parent's proper role is not to control but to help the child establish control. Like teaching a child any other skill, toilet training requires leadership and clear demonstration of positive authority (a demonstration that communicates confidence to the child). Brazelton's advice is not consistent with that objective. The problem is twofold: He advocates waiting long past the window of maximum opportunity has opened and shut, and he undermines the authority and confidence parents must carry into the process to make it go smoothly. In other words, even if Brazelton believed as I do that the time to toilet train is between eighteen and twenty-four months, parents who followed his advice would still have problems because his advice fails to affirm and strengthen a proper parental attitude.

For example, and by contrast, I believe that if a child shows resistance, the parent should calmly stay the course. I believe that if a child has an accident, which is inevitable, the parent should calmly stay the course. I even believe that if the child shows fear, the parent should calmly stay the course. I believe parents know what is best for children. I believe parents should empathize with the irrational fears that children sometimes manifest, but I also believe they should not let a child's irrational fears define the course of his upbringing or any aspect of it.

Naked and $75

Actually, my method isn't *my* method at all. It's a variant of a traditional method of toilet training used by mothers in developing countries. A young woman from India told me it was exactly how her grandmother described toilet training her mother.

I give it a name her grandmother didn't use: "Naked and $75." As the term implies, the child is naked from the waist down. The $75 is the cost of cleaning your carpets when the process is complete, which generally takes no more than a few weeks. Again, the best time to begin is between eighteen and twenty-four months, but my daughter-in-law Nancy used it to train her first child in about a week when he was two-and-one-half—a week before his first sibling was born!

When *you're* ready (the only readiness sign you should heed), buy a child's potty and tell your child he's no longer going to wear diapers during the day. Instead, he's going to put his (insert favorite euphemisms) in his potty, which you have strategically placed in the area of the home in which he spends most of his time. Yes, even if it's the kitchen! The potty needs to be readily available for obvious reasons, but also so that it will serve as a constant visual reminder of the new expectation. Tell him that if he needs help he should just call for you.

Until success is achieved, if your child is a girl, have her wear something similar to a nightshirt around the house. If a boy, put him in the thinnest cotton underwear you can find. Why? Because although children are content to release into their diapers, they do not like it when the substances run down their legs. When that happens, they stand stock still, spread their legs, and yell for help. When you hear this distress, go to your child, restate your expectations, and help him clean up. Stay calm and be positive, but do not tell him that his accident is okay.

During the week or two that this method typically takes, keep your distance. Do not repeatedly ask your child if he has to use the potty. Nothing is more counterproductive to successful training than a hovering, anxious parent. When your child is using the toilet successfully, spend $75 (more or less) to have your carpets cleaned. Believe me, the stains are not permanent, and the cleaning process will even remove any lingering smells. (You might consider not throwing any dinner parties during the training period.) From that point on, you can slowly but surely graduate your child from naked to underpants (not bulky training pants or those nefarious garments known as pull-ups!) and later to full dress.

Despair not, working parents! If you initiate training on a Friday evening and focus on nothing else through the weekend, you'll probably be close to getting over the hump by Sunday evening. If need be, take a couple of days off work to complete the process.

There you have it, a tried-and-true, hassle-free method that involves only one readiness sign: *You* are ready to stop changing diapers. "Naked and $75" is truly child oriented because it respects a child's intelligence and his right to begin taking control of himself and his life as early as reasonably possible.

Voilà!

Attachment
Babble

*"A person with a new idea is a crank
until the idea succeeds."*

—MARK TWAIN

Attachment parenting is a prime example of how parenting experts turn worthwhile theory into babble. Attachment theory, first advanced by British developmental psychologist John Bowlby in the early 1950s, posits that in order for a child to eventually become a mentally healthy adult, during infancy and early childhood he must experience "a warm, intimate, and continuous relationship with his mother (or permanent mother substitute) in which both find satisfaction and enjoyment." Bowlby's almost exclusive focus on the mother's role was a reflection of his early training in Freudian theory. Like most other psychologists of that era, Bowlby thought that a father's influence was virtually insignificant; the typical father was a bystander in his child's development.

Whether a warm, intimate, mutually satisfying mother–child relationship is as essential to later mental health as Bowlby contended is open to debate, but sensible people would agree that given the alternative, it is certainly the preferable state of affairs. In other words, Bowlby simply recognized what common sense would affirm. He went on to do excellent field research (based primarily on observation rather than comparison between an experimental and control group) into both grief and separation anxiety during infancy and early childhood.

One of Bowlby's students, Mary Ainsworth, conducted equally excellent field research in Uganda and Baltimore and came to the conclusion that a mother's appropriate sensitivity to the needs of her young child provided a secure foundation that enabled confident exploration of the environment, facilitated problem solving, and encouraged independence. Later researchers, including psychologist Burton White, author of *The First Three Years of Life*, have discovered pretty much the same connection between the quality of maternal care and developmental health.

Subsequent research has questioned whether adequate attachment depends exclusively on the mother, and there is now evidence that the gender of the primary attachment figure is not as critical as Bowlby and Ainsworth believed. Rather, what seems crucial is a committed caregiving relationship with one or even more than one adults. It now appears that infants bond equally well with mothers or fathers (or mother or father substitutes) as long as the adults in question are loving, attentive, reasonably available, and appropriately responsive to the child's needs.

It is important to note that none of Bowlby's or Ainsworth's research-based conclusions were inconsistent with common sense and common parenting practice. Nor did either of them recommend radical parenting practices such as prolonged breastfeeding or so-called co-sleeping—parents and children sleeping in the same bed. But this is precisely the exaggerated direction in which their theories have been taken by various post-1960s parenting experts.

The History of Attachment Parenting, Part 1

In 1975, self-taught cultural anthropologist Jean Liedloff wrote *The Continuum Concept,* the book that is usually cited as the primary inspiration for the rise of the attachment parenting movement. As a young woman, Liedloff joined a diamond-hunting expedition in the Venezuelan jungle, where she encountered a primitive tribe known as the Yequana (also Yekwana or Yecuana). Over the course of several trips, she became increasingly fascinated with their communal Stone Age culture and wound up living with them for a time.

Liedloff became convinced that the Yequana style of child rearing was far superior to that typical of Western parents. Yequana children played happily, performed chores willingly at early ages, never quarreled, and seemed much more competent at a much earlier age than their Euro-American counterparts. Liedloff was also impressed by the fact that the kids in question were left pretty much unsupervised while adults went about their daily tasks.

Her observations led her to begin questioning the practices and the basic assumptions of Western child rearing. She eventually came to the conclusion that Western culture has developed into a mass pathology supported by dysfunctional parenting attitudes and practices that force a distorted definition of normality on children, at the same time causing them to deny and repress their true nature.

One of Liedloff's key observations was that the Yequana infant was almost constantly carried by and in skin contact with its mother, who breastfed on demand until her child was at least three. In Western culture, because that practice is virtually nonexistent and even frowned upon, Liedloff believed that an adversarial relationship quickly develops between parent and child. The result is a baby, and then a child, who cries frequently (is excessively demanding), throws tantrums (reflecting a lack of tolerance for frustration), refuses to cooperate with instructions, is defiant, and so on. In Liedloff's view, all child misbehavior was simply an expression of the child's true nature being denied by the culture, which demanded that parents raise children who would become willing soldiers in the constant march of "progress."

In a 1998 interview, Liedloff said, "It's perfectly clear that the millions of babies who are crying at this very moment want unanimously to be next to a live body. Do you really think they're all wrong? Theirs is the voice of nature. This is the clear, pure voice of nature, without intellectual interference."

Quite obviously, Liedloff came to the conclusion that the Yequana culture represented a human utopia that managed to raise its children without sin (the Judeo-Christian perspective) or psychological problems (the secular perspective). In fact, she came to believe that human beings were innately good and that in Western culture, the child's original pure nature was sullied by child-rearing practices that served the needs of the state and the industrial economy but were in direct opposition to the needs of the child. Hers was a fascinating theory that fit nicely with the demonization of Western civilization that had begun on college campuses in the 1960s and continues there even today. Whether she was right or wrong, Liedloff's thesis had a built-in guarantee of popularity, especially among young baby boomers who had jumped on the "Let's destroy bad old Western civilization and build a perfect society on the rubble" bandwagon that was careening through the United States and Europe at the time.

Ironically, Liedloff had only scorn for parenting experts, but she ultimately invented herself as one. Like Thomas Gordon, Dorothy Briggs, and other rising experts of the era, Liedloff believed she had been given unique insights that enabled her to see all that was wrong about Western child rearing and to know how to make things right again. Central to her child-rearing plan was what she called "the continuum concept," the idea that in order to develop properly, children needed the sort of rearing experience that *Homo sapiens* had worked out during its long evolution, including:

◆ Constant physical contact with the mother from birth until the child begins crawling.

◆ Sleeping with parents, in their bed, until he leaves of his own volition.

◆ Breastfeeding on demand until age three.

◆ Caretakers who respond immediately to any sign of discomfort.

In Liedloff's view, when the child's built-in (instinctual) "continuum expectations" are adequately responded to and satisfied, he develops a natural sense of well-being, self-assuredness, and joy at being alive. Liedloff decried such Western childbirth and child-rearing practices as separating the child and mother almost immediately after delivery (rarely done today), isolating the child in his own bed and letting him cry himself to sleep, rigid feeding schedules (not recommended by the American Academy of Pediatrics), ignoring crying between feedings, excluding the child from adult activities, the use of playpens, and the use of punishment in response to misbehavior. In response to these counterevolutionary practices, Liedloff believed the child develops a sense of "wrongness" and shame toward himself. A world populated by such shame-filled people is an unpleasant place where people compensate by either doing what they are told or attempting to acquire power over others. This concept of "shame-based" parenting was echoed by Gordon, Briggs, Faber, and others. In the 1970s and 1980s, for example, motivational speaker John Bradshaw, author of *Healing the Shame That Binds You,* enjoyed considerable popularity for his notion that traditional American parenting practices were inherently shame inducing.

Interestingly, Liedloff and I agree that the proper parent–child arrangement is one in which the child pays attention to adults and wants to learn from them. We also agree that parents should do as little for a child as possible, allowing him to figure out things for himself by trial and error. This libertarian style of parenting sends the child the important message that he is capable of solving his own problems without much adult assistance. I completely approve, although I do not believe—and neither impartial research nor experience confirms it—that development of this sense of self-competence requires the sort of attachment parenting that Liedloff described.

I have long maintained that child-rearing attitudes and resulting practices define culture. In this regard, the question of why the Yequana were still a Stone Age culture in the 1950s is pertinent. The answer is likely to be found in child-rearing practices that endowed children with a sturdy sense of well-being and the feeling that everything in the world was as it should be but did not encourage questioning, creativity, or innovation. For reasons that were no doubt highly personal, Liedloff romanticized and idealized the Yequana and made the mistake of believing that their child-rearing customs could be exported successfully to a technologically advanced society. But again, when considering Liedloff's thesis, one must keep in mind that she had fundamental problems with Western civilization. In the same 1998 interview cited earlier, she characterized Western society as "unpleasant, dangerous, unhappy, alienated, and unstable," all of which she thought could be remedied if we used a Stone Age tribe as our parenting role model.

The History of Attachment Parenting, Part 2

Jean Liedloff's impact on post-1960s parenting culture is almost equal to Thomas Gordon's. Her writings attracted numerous disciples who spread the gospel of Paleolithic parenting far and wide. The first to jump on Liedloff's bandwagon was Minnesota homemaker Tine Thevenin. In her 1976 book *The Family Bed,* Thevenin advanced the notion that the child who grows up happy and emotionally healthy is the child who, from infancy, is allowed to sleep in the same bed with his or her parents until such time as he decides to sleep separately, regardless of age.

Upon its release, *The Family Bed* was praised by attachment parenting advocates and groups such as La Leche League because of its emphasis on mother–baby bonding and the importance of breastfeeding on cue, even throughout the night. In making her case for parents and little ones bedding together, Thevenin pointed to anthropological studies of numerous societies in which children slept with their parents. In particular, she highlighted the living habits of the Okinawan indigenous people. She noted that Okinawan children sleep next to their parents on the same mat until they are six years old. At age six, they are moved on to another sleeping arrangement. According to Thevenin, the Okinawan people enjoy a greater sense of inner security, emotional stability, tranquility, contentment, and personal well-being than Westerners. She attributes this to the "basic security received from their infancy." Thus, Thevenin echoed Liedloff's message: If you want to raise your kids right, follow the example of villagers in rural South America or Asia, where culture has not progressed beyond the Stone Age.

The family bed is a cozy arrangement for sure, but it puts the parent–child relationship front and center and the marriage on the back burner. It also involves the risk of having children who do not want to leave their parents' bed, ever. Over the years, I've counseled many parents who regretted ever embracing the family bed. They generally came to me asking how to get children as old as eight to sleep cooperatively in their own beds. In other words, cozy can turn into a nightmare. One such tale involved a mother who came to me about her three-year-old daughter's habit of waking up several times a night, screaming for Mommy to sleep with her. On those occasions, the child often came into her parents' room, disrupting the entire family because that was where her infant sibling slept, occupying the coveted place that had been hers until she was two and said sibling was born.

The mother reported that as infants and young toddlers the children slept in the parents' bed because it was easier for her to nurse. Three years into this arrangement, she and her husband were both sleep deprived and often reacted angrily to their older child's nightly transgressions. She realized that their frustration wasn't making matters any better, and she said that in their more rational states of mind she and her husband promised their three-year-old daughter candy and fish for her fish tank if she'd just let them get a good night's sleep. Needless to say, their daughter did not appreciate these "rational" moments. This is the sort of completely unnecessary problem often created by co-sleeping. Common sense says that if these children had been in their own beds from birth, the problem would never have arisen.

Family bed proponents claim it assists with bonding and attachment and other such nonsense, but no study by an impartial party has found any lasting benefit to it. The fact is that children who sleep with their parents don't learn how to put themselves to sleep and stay asleep, just as children who use pacifiers don't learn how to comfort themselves. In both cases, the ability of a child to self-soothe is important to his learning that he can solve his own problems.

Problems of the sort described by this mother are typical when parents try to move a co-sleeping child into his or her own bed. In other words, having a child in bed with you during infancy and early toddlerhood may "solve" the bedtime hassles sometimes associated with the age. But co-sleeping often leads to even worse sleep problems, just as pacifiers often lead to tantrums, excessive crying, and petulance.

The second, equally important issue is boundaries. The discipline of a child is accomplished through the effective conveyance of parent leadership, and effective leadership requires a boundary between the leader and the led. In the case of the parent–child equation, the boundary should be permeable, but the parent absolutely must control when and how often the child is allowed through it. The sanctity of the marital bed is Boundary Number One. When that does not exist, establishing any other boundaries will be extremely difficult, which is why I have found that co-sleeping and discipline problems go pretty much hand in hand (although I have observed that co-sleeping parents are often in denial about these discipline problems).

In this case, I recommended that the parents move the infant out of the marital bed, not only to head off later sleep problems with this second child but also to set the stage for the next step: a definitive, boundary-setting talk with the three-year-old. I instructed Mom and Dad to sit her down and inform her that when they told her doctor that her brother was sleeping in their bed, "He told us that no child can sleep in our bed. He also told us that you must not get up in the night crying, because we can't get in bed with you either. You have to stay in your bed all night long, just like other children do. To help you remember, we're putting a gate in your doorway. If you wake up at night, you can turn on a light and play in your room, but your doctor says you must be very quiet so that Mommy and Daddy don't wake up. If you wake us up, your doctor says we have to put you back in your bed, and he says you can't (insert something the child enjoys doing every day), and you have to go to bed early the next night."

Why blame it on the doctor? Because at this point the child recognizes and will comply readily with the doctor's authority, so he or she is used as a transitional authority figure until the parents have their leadership feet on solid ground.

My experience with this nonreward, nonpunitive approach is that some children take to it almost immediately, but others put up the fight of their lives for two to three weeks. That's actually a small price to pay, given where this situation might otherwise go.

The History of Attachment Parenting, Part 3

By far the most prominent of Liedloff's disciples, California pediatrician Dr. Bill Sears, is credited with coining the term *attachment parenting*. Sears and his wife, Martha, a registered nurse, have co-authored twelve books, including the two "bibles" of the attachment parenting movement, *The Baby Book* (1993) and *The Attachment Parenting Book* (2001).

For the Searses, it is crucial that mothers learn to read their babies so they can attach as early and sufficiently as possible. To accomplish that, they advocate seven parenting principles they regard as essential to proper mother–child bonding. These "Baby B's," as they call them, have become a virtual mantra in the attachment parenting movement:

◆ *Birth bonding*. Mothers should hold their babies, nurse their babies, and let their babies experience skin-to-skin contact immediately after delivery.

◆ *Breastfeeding*. Mothers should nurse their babies, preferably well into toddlerhood or until the child naturally weans.

◆ *Baby wearing*. Mothers (and fathers) should "wear" their babies in a sling when not carrying them in their arms in order to keep them close, feeling secure, and in a state of "quiet alertness" so they can observe what their parents are doing and begin to learn the rituals and routines of their families.

- *Bedding down close to baby.* Mothers should sleep with their babies in the same bed.

- *Belief in baby's cries.* Parents should interpret their baby's cries as communicating a need rather than as a demand for attention, and they should respond accordingly by holding and nursing the child right away as opposed to letting the child cry it out.

- *Beware of baby trainers.* The Searses warn parents about "using someone else's training method to get your baby to sleep or get your baby on a predictable schedule. Most of these methods are variations of the tired old theme of letting baby cry it out." They claim that parents who let their infants cry themselves to sleep run the risk of becoming "desensitized" to their children's cues.

- *Balance in parenting.* The Searses warn against mommies giving so much of themselves to their children that they neglect their own needs and their marriages.

Basing his claims predominantly on his own personal and professional experience and testimonials from other attachment parenting parents rather than impartial research, Sears proposes that his approach to child rearing "immunizes children against many of the social and emotional diseases that plague our society." He goes on to promise parents who adopt his method that they will develop the wisdom they need to make proper decisions for their children and that their children will turn out better than children raised otherwise.

By "turn out better" Sears means a child who is more intelligent, calm, secure, socially confident, empathic, and independent than a child raised according to prevailing Western norms. He even promises that attachment parenting will result in a child who doesn't tell lies. On his Web site, in an essay titled "11 Ways to Raise a Truthful Child," he writes, "Connected children do not become habitual liars. They trust their caregivers and have such a good self-image they don't need to lie." He doesn't support this with any hard evidence obtained using the scientific method (an experiment involving both a control group and an experimental group) because there is no such evidence.

Sears's Web site and writings are full of overblown, indefensible claims of this sort. To cite another example, he says that the hormone prolactin, which performs or assists in numerous biological functions including stimulating milk production (lactation), "further enhances (a woman's) mothering behavior." Nothing of this sort is attributed to prolactin in any of the medical literature I consulted. By claiming this benefit, Sears implies that a woman who doesn't breastfeed her baby is less effective than the woman who does, that she is selling her baby short, depriving him of essential biological and psychic gifts, and so on. This is pure, unadulterated hogwash. Although both the American Pediatric Society and American Medical Association recommend breastfeeding for at least the first six months, and although there are established medical benefits of breastfeeding (see Kidshealth.org), there is no conclusive evidence that breastfeeding produces significant emotional, behavioral, or intellectual benefits or that breastfed children turn out better.

For Sears and other attachment parenting advocates, it's essential that mothers get and remain "connected" to their children. What constitutes this state of "connectedness," and by what measure does one know it has properly formed? These are questions Sears never answers because he can't. In fact, he never gives any objective data or evidence to support any of his contentions. For example, he claims, "Researchers at Stanford University found that babies settle best when held by caregivers who move in all planes of motion" but fails—conveniently?—to cite his source. I was unable to find reference to any such research. And what exactly does Sears mean by a caregiver who moves "in all planes of motion"? Is he simply referring to moving in three-dimensional space, which is what three-dimensional beings cannot help but do?

On his Web site, under "Attachment Research," Sears refers to but one study done in 1972 in which the number of parents involved was not sufficient for drawing any conclusions other than that babies are far better off being raised by mothers who are interested in and responsive to them than they are being raised by uninterested, unresponsive mothers. Did we need a research study to know that? Most research confirms that it is impossible to pay too much attention to a baby. But that does not justify breastfeeding until age three or sleeping with one's child until he finally, at age thirteen, tells you he's ready for his own bed. And by the way, I've heard from quite a number of parents who slept with their children into their teen years. Even if it was possible to show that attachment parenting practices produce significant long-term benefits—which no unbiased researcher has found—for adults to sleep in the same bed with a pubescent teen is highly inappropriate, especially when an alternative is readily available.

Sears consistently appeals to sentimental emotion. Two examples:

◆ Mom will know that she has connected by a "feeling of rightness" between herself and her baby. One would suppose, therefore, that postpartum depression is evidence that the mother has failed at connecting and establishing this feeling of rightness. Yet there is no evidence that children of moms with postpartum depression are at higher risk of later intellectual, emotional, or social difficulties than kids whose moms did not experience this very real and very debilitating condition.

◆ On his Web site, Sears says that attachment parenting is "opening your mind and heart to the individual needs of your baby." Does this mean that mothers who do not practice attachment parenting—who, for example, go back to full-time jobs as soon as possible—have minds and hearts that are not responsive to the needs of their babies? This is anti-intellectual drivel.

To be fair, there is truth in some of what Sears says. Research shows that there are health benefits to breastfeeding, but it does not show that bottle-fed babies are at significant risk of any emotional or physical problem in the short or long term. Most (but not all) of an early infant's cries express true need states, but research does not show that babies who are fed on schedule rather than on demand are at emotional risk. Moms and dads do need to respond to their infants so as to assure them that they are going to be provided for, protected, and loved under any and all circumstances, but no research exists to suggest this is possible only with attachment parenting. Yes, the first year of a baby's life will require a great deal of responsive attention, mostly from Mom, but research does not find that the only effective way to provide this attention is to practice attachment parenting. In short, many if not all of Sears's claims are unproven; some even fly in the face of sound scientific research, historical evidence, and common sense.

Is Attachment Parenting a Cult?

A young mother who identified herself as a practitioner of attachment parenting approached me after I'd given a talk in Nashville and told me that "children should be approached with reverence." In her view, my parenting philosophy denied the child's worthiness as an object of worshipful adoration. (One of the primary characteristics of a cult is idolatry, the exaggerated veneration of a material thing or person in place of a higher supernatural being or power.) She was correct, in fact. Because they are inclined by their nature to choose self-serving behavior over behavior that is primarily respectful of the rights and feelings of others, children need firm, purposeful discipline from adults who love them unconditionally and regard them compassionately. But said love and compassion should not cross the line into reverence. Children are self-centered enough without that.

I subsequently learned that this young woman was a member of the Tennessee chapter of Attachment Parenting International and that when chapter leaders learned of my upcoming presentation, she and the chapter president had tried to persuade the sponsoring organization to cancel the talk and substitute someone they approved of. (Another characteristic of a cult is that its members, and especially its leaders, are highly threatened, often to the point of paranoia, by ideas that oppose their own and use whatever means available to suppress those ideas so that existing or potential cult members are not exposed to them.)

Over the past few years, a significant number of former attachment parenting adherents have told me that membership in attachment parenting support groups took over their lives. They socialized almost exclusively with other group members, their conversations revolved around group beliefs and practices, and consequently they became obsessed with correctly conforming to group orthodoxy. (Cults discourage socializing with outsiders and encourage members to make cult practices a major feature, if not the major feature, of their lives.)

These same women told me they were afraid to admit to other support group members that they occasionally fed their children from bottles, pushed them in strollers, or let them cry themselves to sleep in their own cribs or beds. (Cult membership always involves tremendous peer pressure to conform rigidly and obsessively to a set of beliefs or practices that are outside the mainstream.)

These same women have also told me that when they began to seriously question attachment parenting orthodoxy, they were promptly "excommunicated" from their support groups or excluded from certain group activities. When they finally left their support groups, none of the remaining mothers would have anything to do with them. (Cults are quick to expel and then isolate any member who begins to violate or even question group orthodoxy.) Because these heretics might begin to sway the thinking of other members, they have to be expelled.

Attachment parenting organizations, from local mother support groups to Attachment Parenting International, exhibit characteristics that define a cult. In this regard, I have spoken to or heard from a number of former attachment parenting moms who used the term *cult* in recounting their experiences. These moms described in highly negative terms the peer pressure they felt to conform their mothering behavior to the inflexible "correctness" of attachment parenting orthodoxy: to never bottle feed, even if their breasts were sore or out of milk; to always carry their babies, even if it was inconvenient or they were physically exhausted; to sleep with their children, even if doing so brought on sleep deprivation or caused serious marital conflict; and so on. (In the final analysis, cult leaders care more about people adhering to doctrine than they do about the people themselves.)

I conclude that attachment parenting, and especially membership in attachment parenting support groups, is decidedly unhealthy for women, whether they realize it or not. Many disaffected former members have affirmed that to me. Needless to say, current attachment parenting support group members are outraged at the suggestion. When these adherents are asked to explain the criticisms of former members, the usual answer is that "attachment parenting isn't for everyone."

But wait! That's their central point, isn't it? That attachment parenting is the *only* proper way to raise a child; that there is no acceptable alternative; that any other form of parenting puts a child at risk? I suspect that "attachment parenting isn't for everyone" really means that not every mother has what it takes to measure up to the standards, that some mothers are just too self-absorbed or lazy or irresponsible, or their priorities are too out of whack, or they're just too ignorant. There's a pronounced self-righteousness to this attachment parenting business—the sense that its practitioners are members of a parenting elite that is willing to make the sacrifices necessary to ensure the well-being of their kids—a distinct and malodorous emanation of superiority.

But is there really any compelling, concrete evidence that attachment parenting lives up to its promises?

Does Attachment Parenting Really Grow Better Kids?

The answer is no. Diana Baumrind's parenting research (reviewed in chapter two) finds that a combination of unconditional love and firm discipline produces the most well-adjusted kids. Except for unconditional love, which goes without saying, Baumrind's description of optimal parenting style is not at all congruent with attachment parenting practice.

Breast milk is undoubtedly more nutritious than formula, but today's formulas are very close approximations of breast milk and cannot, by any stretch, be accused of being unhealthy for babies. Breast milk probably provides more effective immunity during infancy and toddlerhood, and it is nonallergenic, but one should keep in mind that attachment parenting proponents claim that breastfeeding provides a child with long-term emotional advantages. Absolutely no good, reliable data exist to support a claim of that sort. A highly trained child psychologist observing a group of young children playing together would not be able to differentiate the ones who were breastfed from the ones who were not. By age five, a breastfed kid could be just as pleasant or just as insufferable as one who was bottle fed.

As for co-sleeping, the actual meaning of the term is becoming blurred to include both bed sharing and sleeping in the same room but not in the same bed. For clarity, I will use the terms *bed sharing* and *room sharing*. Research finds that when infants sleep in the same room (but not in the same bed) as their parents, the risk of sudden infant death syndrome (SIDS)—the umbrella term for all unexplained infant deaths that occur while sleeping—is cut by one-half. When babies sleep in the same rooms with their parents, night-time crying is reduced, breastfeeding is made easier, and mothers are likely to breastfeed longer. These are all distinct advantages, but mind you, they do not require bed sharing, nor do they require that parents adhere to attachment parenting doctrine.

James J. McKenna, director of the Mother–Baby Behavioral Sleep Laboratory at Notre Dame University, claims that co-sleeping (which he uses to include both bed sharing and room sharing) results in superior cognitive ability at age six and greater problem-solving independence during toddlerhood. He also claims to have found that young adults who slept with their parents as infants and young children were more satisfied with their bodies and had more secure gender identities. I have looked at the data in question and find it to be inconclusive. It appears to me that McKenna may have crossed the line from researcher to activist, a hazard of doing social science research. Rather than maintaining a dispassionate position concerning the subject, McKenna has become an advocate of bed sharing. To cite one example, he says that in those cultures where bed sharing rates are the highest, rates of SIDS are lowest. In an online article titled "Cosleeping and Biological Imperatives: Why Human Babies Do Not and Should Not Sleep Alone," McKenna argues with the recommendation from the American Academy of Pediatrics (AAP) that parents and infants sleep in separate beds. He even suggests it was immoral for the AAP to tell a mother that no matter how responsible she is, her body is in effect a "potential lethal weapon." Yet the research clearly supports the recommendation. A 2012 meta-analysis of eleven controlled studies, cited by the AAP in its policy statement on the issue, found that children who bed share with their parents are three times as likely to die of SIDS as infants who sleep alone.

No rational person would deny that there are important short-term practical advantages to babies sleeping in the same room with their parents (and by the way, the AAP recommends room sharing during early infancy). I maintain, however, that those advantages do not significantly increase when a baby is in the parents' bed. Furthermore, I would argue that while it is relatively easy to move a room-sharing six-month-old to another sleeping room, it is very difficult to move a bed-sharing six-month-old to another bed. In most cases, the former has already learned how to put himself to sleep on his own, called self-soothing. The latter has not. Moving him out of his parents' bed is going to cause him significant distress. His parents are likely to respond by bringing him back into their bed, not realizing that this is going to make future attempts at moving him even more difficult. At some point, the child's presence in the marital bed is likely to become disruptive to the marriage.

In 2012, former child actress Mayim Bialik became the poster mom for attachment parenting with the publication of *Beyond the Sling*, which was part memoir, part advocacy. In it, she describes her family's sleeping arrangement: She and her husband go to bed and sleep with their two young boys on futons laid side by side on the floor. She admits that she and her husband never have sex in bed anymore. Nevertheless, she goes on to praise the mother–child advantages of this unconventional arrangement. It would seem that being "bonded" with her children is more important to her than intimacy with her husband. Who knows, this may be acceptable to her husband; but I've talked with lots of husbands who did not know what they were getting into when they agreed to bed share with their kids and who testify to growing marital difficulties as a result.

McKenna also says that the benefits of co-sleeping are verified by his own and others' "refereed [subject to rigorous peer review], published scientific research." Once again, it appears that he conveniently ignores evidence to the contrary. For example, a 2002 study out of the University of California, Los Angeles, and published in the *Journal of Developmental and Behavior Pediatrics,* found that by age eighteen, children who had slept with their parents showed no advantage over children who had slept alone. The variables measured included social skills, drug and alcohol use, antisocial behavior, and overall psychological well-being. I'm reasonably certain that this study was refereed before it was published, meaning it had to pass rigorous peer review.

Dr. Alice Callahan, who writes a blog at scienceofmom.com, has carried out an extensive review of the literature pertaining to methods of training infants to fall asleep on their own and put themselves back to sleep when they wake (known as self-soothing). She concludes that sleep training results in reduced bedtime struggles, fewer night wakings, and longer sleep periods for both baby and parents. Also, mothers of sleep-trained babies were less likely to experience postpartum depression. Parents reported improved baby temperament and mood, less overall parenting stress, greater confidence, and—no surprise here—greater marital satisfaction. Callahan writes that "of all the studies of sleep training, not a single one has identified a negative effect on babies' behavior or relationship with caregivers."

Interestingly, these results are irrespective of the form of sleep training used, including letting babies cry themselves to sleep. Since the 1970s, I've been advising parents through my books and syndicated newspaper column to use what is now known as "graduated extinction." This involves parents periodically calming the crying child and increasing the comforting interval over succeeding nights. Although the research doesn't confirm the superiority of this method of sleep training, I think most parents prefer it over letting children "cry it out."

In summary, when one looks at the total body of research into infant and child sleep, the contention that bed sharing is superior to solo sleep seems impossible to objectively defend.

Bonding versus Boundaries

The real, verifiable problem with co-sleeping is that it prevents the establishment of effective boundaries between mother and child and between marriage and child. During a child's first two years of life, it is almost impossible during her child's waking hours for a mother to establish a relationship boundary. She has to be constantly attentive and responsive to her child. (Note: This state of vigilance and sensitivity does not require that a mother carry her child around all day in a sling.) Around the second birthday, Mom needs to begin establishing that boundary and adjusting her child's expectations of her. For her sake as well as her child's, she needs to communicate that she is not at his beck and call, his servant, on-demand playmate, or "gofer" of any sort.

Both she and her husband, who has been somewhat on the sidelines during those first two years, now need to be seen by the child as authority figures (their primary role from age three to thirteen, which I call the decade of discipline) and reestablish their marriage at the center of the family. For one person to effect proper, ethical authority over someone else demands a boundary between the person delivering the authority and its recipient or beneficiary. The boundary in question should be permeable, but the parent should be in charge of determining the degree of permeability at any time.

Attachment parenting is an arrangement that prevents establishment of that essential boundary. In fact, attachment parenting doctrine effectively *forbids* the mother from establishing that boundary, thus making it almost impossible for her child to see her as an authority figure and understand the need to obey her. This translates into unnecessary stress for attachment parenting mothers, most of whom deny any stress until they leave the cult, at which time they confess to having been under near-constant stress.

The lack of mother–child boundary hinders the child's ability to learn how to solve his own problems, including playing by himself. In that regard, developmental psychologist Burton White, author of *The First Three Years of Life,* has said that the primary marker of good developmental health in a three-year-old is the child's ability to entertain himself for an hour or more at a time without asking for adult assistance or attention. Needless to say, it is impossible for a mother to help a child get along without her constant attention if she feels compelled to pay constant attention. Likewise, it is impossible for a mother to teach a child to self-entertain if she feels compelled to be involved in his every activity, at his every waking moment. Attachment parenting mentors, including chief attachment parenting guru Dr. Bill Sears, say this is not what attachment parenting is all about, but they must not be getting their point across very effectively. The typical attachment parenting mother is found talking to, playing with, helping, serving, and generally attending to her child, regardless of the child's age, virtually around the clock, until the child enters school.

The lack of boundary means that the mother is likely to experience raising her child as a state of near-constant demand. Many former attachment parenting moms have told me that they began to feel suffocated by their children's near-constant demands for attention and guilty when they did not comply. In short, a preponderance of evidence from former attachment parenting practitioners strongly suggests that attachment parenting results in the "attached" child being in control of the parent–child relationship.

It is also vital to the health of the family unit that the husband–wife relationship be more energetic than the relationship between either of the parents and the child. A marriage-centered family unit is in the best interests of all concerned. It greatly improves the quality of the husband–wife relationship and significantly reduces the risk of divorce. In addition, it puts a platform of security underneath a child for which no real substitute exists. After all, there is nothing that so grounds a child, so ensures his sense of well-being, as knowing that his parents are in a committed relationship. Co-sleeping prevents reestablishing the marriage at the center of the family, a process that should begin around the second birthday and be completed by the third. Here's the testimony of Raed Rihani, a mother who discovered all of this the hard way:

This book [Sears' The Attachment Parenting Book] should come with a warning! When we first started with this book we were very excited about it and bought copies for all of our friends who were having children. Almost four years later, all of us are suffering from the same thing. Intimacy is a very important aspect of a healthy marriage, and let's face it, a child in your bed for three-plus years isn't going to help your cause. Dr. Sears writes that children will eventually want to sleep on their own sometime after the age of two. Our first child is three years and eight months old now and we just got him moved to his own room. However, I'm sleeping with him until our second child (now two months old) is old enough to replace me (we hope). Every effort to get him to sleep in his own bed has been met with fierce resistance. At the end of the day, I don't blame him! There is no way to get a child who's become comfortable sleeping with Mom and Dad to willingly start sleeping in their own bed without causing some emotional distress.

Rihani's comments echo those of hundreds of former attachment parenting parents who have communicated their disaffection to me over the years. That, along with the significant number of clinical psychologists and family therapists who've told me about the disciplinary and dependency issues they regularly encounter in attachment parented children, adds up to a certified parenting fiasco or, more accurately perhaps, a farce. There is no scientifically valid, confirmed evidence that any attachment parenting practice leads to any reliable long-term positive outcome. Yet attachment parenting proponents such as Dr. William Sears continue to blur and misrepresent the facts, claiming all manner of amazing benefits for both parent and child. I conclude that attachment parenting is the parenting equivalent of snake oil.

The Antidote

Healthy parenting is quite simple, actually. It's obvious that human beings share with other mammals a strong instinct toward species preservation and perpetuation. We want our children to thrive, to be healthy, to get the best possible start in life. We take great pride in seeing our kids become creative, well-behaved children; then confident, well-mannered teenagers; then responsible adults. Nurturing and guiding that process requires a significant investment of time and energy, especially during a child's early years. But it is self-evident that for parents to raise a child to responsible adulthood does not require that they practice attachment parenting according to Liedloff and Sears.

From the beginning, children need healthful diets. It is undeniable that breast milk is the ideal food for infants, at least until they are capable of eating solid food. In this day and age, however, children in advanced cultures do not *need* to be breastfed. And the breastfed child does not need to be breastfed until age three to derive maximum benefit. Six to nine months will do, and if a mother is not able to breastfeed or simply doesn't feel like it, that's fine. That's not reason for guilt. Nor is it reason for a breastfeeding mom to feel any guilt. By the time these two kids are three years old, no educated observer will be able to tell which is which.

Children need attention, and babies need a lot of attention. But once a child is walking, he needs more supervision than he does attention. Until he can anticipate potential danger on his own, his parents need to make sure he's not getting into trouble. The most time-efficient way of doing that is to childproof the home. Because I've delved into the how-to of that process sufficiently in other books (most notably *The New Parent Power!*), I won't go into details here. I will say only that childproofing prevents parents from hovering and frustrating themselves and their children. In the final analysis, however, it's as wrong to say that children need a lot of attention as it is to say they need a lot of food. They need both, but just as a child can become dependent on food, a child can become dependent on adult attention. The trick is to find the point of "just enough" and stay there. The food–attention analogy breaks down with age, however. As a child gets older, he needs more food to sustain a growing body. But as a child gets older, he should need less and less attention as well as less and less supervision.

Children need sleep. In fact, sleep deprivation during childhood has become a major problem because children's bedrooms have become self-contained entertainment complexes jammed with all manner of aural and visual stimulation. The research indicates that babies need to sleep around sixteen hours a day, toddlers around fourteen, preschool children at least twelve, school-age kids at least ten, and teens at least eight. Insufficient sleep interferes with attentiveness, lowers task performance, causes irritability and generally low tolerance for frustration, and can even result in serious emotional problems such as pervasive anxiety and depression if prolonged. All that aside, it is not necessary for parents to sleep with children, and no impartial research finds any long-term benefit to children associated with parent–child co-sleeping.

However, it does not take research to figure out that parent–child co-sleeping can eventually result in a sleep-deprived parent. The quality of one's sleep experience will be significantly reduced by the constant presence and position of a baby in the same bed. And don't forget that the number of children in bed with the parent is not likely to stop at one. As more kids come along, the complications of parent–child co-sleeping obviously increase. That's why, in many attachment parenting families, Mom sleeps in one bed with one or two kids, and Dad sleeps in another bed, usually in another bedroom, with one or two kids. Excuse me, but that's just wrong.

There is obvious benefit to a marriage when husband and wife sleep together in the same bed, without children squirming around in between them. The healthiest family is a marriage-centered family. The healthiest family is one in which husband and wife pay more attention to one another than they do to their kids. That marriage is more likely to last, and the research clearly shows that divorce is not a desirable outcome. Kids benefit from marriage-centeredness as well. First, that arrangement gives them complete permission to grow up and emancipate early and responsibly. Second, in a child's mind, nothing substitutes for the knowledge that Mom and Dad are in a vibrant, permanent relationship with one another. Nothing provides such positive benefit to a child's sense of well-being. Again, the research is clear that good marriages grow healthier children. So don't sleep with your child. Sleep with your mate. The couple who sleeps together, without children in between them, is the couple most likely to stay together, not just physically but emotionally as well.

Sure, put your child in a bassinet or crib in your bedroom for the first several months. Until the child begins sleeping through the night, that closeness has practical advantages, including the fact that you don't have to go far to give the child a bottle or breast. It also means the child cries for a shorter period of time, so both of you will get back to sleep more quickly, which probably means the child will sleep through the night earlier than would otherwise be the case. When he begins sleeping through the night and has done so for a few weeks, move him into his own nicely decorated bedroom and start getting your marriage back.

Children need to be held. They need affection. They need unconditional love. That does not require that they be constantly carried. Lots of research has verified the benefit to children of learning how to self-pacify or self-calm. Those terms refer to children who learn to accept and be at peace with not being in physical touch with a caregiver. Obviously, it's impossible for a child to be at peace with not being in physical contact with a caregiver if the caregiver is constantly in physical contact with the child.

As with separate sleep arrangements, the benefit of mother and child not being in constant contact accrues to both parties. Mom has a child, and she also has a *life*. Under the circumstances, the child becomes autonomous more quickly, and mothering becomes a part-time job more quickly. Everyone benefits!

Healthy parenting is not complicated at all. I don't think anything I've said in this section will strike anyone as strange, but I have to say that most of what is required in order to do "correct" attachment parenting strikes me and many others as strange or, at the very least, completely unnecessary. That so many people have negative reactions to something supposedly natural means it's not natural at all. It also means that attachment parenting and common sense don't mesh. And I believe this: If a parenting "expert" (and this includes me!) says something that doesn't mesh with common sense, one should always go with common sense.

Adoption Babble

*"There is nothing good or bad,
but thinking makes it so."*

—SHAKESPEARE (*HAMLET*)

Adoption has greatly increased over the past forty years. In the 1990s alone, international adoptions of children from Russia, Eastern Europe, China, Latin America, and Southeast Asia by U.S. citizens doubled. Domestic adoptions have also risen dramatically. According to the Adoption Institute, adoptions out of foster care increased 78 percent in the four years from 1996 to 2000.

As adoption has increased, so has adoption babble, and this coincides with the increase in the number of so-called adoption specialists. More often than not, these are folks with degrees in clinical social work or family counseling who work at or through adoption agencies to counsel people who adopt children. In order to justify their vocation (and the number of years they spent in school collecting degrees), these specialists invent blatant myths about the effect of adoption on children. The most prevalent myth is that adopted children come with "attachment issues"; therefore, they have "bonding problems." Oh, and they "grieve," but they just can't put their tiny little fingers on why they are so frequently sad.

To help them come to grips with their grieving, attachment issues, bonding problems, and—oh yes, I almost forgot—abandonment fears and separation anxieties, as well as their anger over being forced against their will to live with strangers, their adoptive parents must talk constantly to them, even when they are infants, about their adoption and make sure to tell them they are special and loved at least ten times a day. The parents must sing adoption songs to them when they go to sleep and read children's books to them about adopted bears who grew up to be happy adult bears and adopted horses who overcame many obstacles and won the Kentucky Derby in spite of it all.

The implication of all this is that adopted children could fall apart at any minute. It's as if nonadopted kids were made out of Lego blocks—they hold together fairly well—but adopted kids were made out of plain, smooth-sided wooden blocks, and the slightest vibration could send them tumbling. Therefore, preadoption and postadoption parent education is a must (this education usually isn't free, by the way), and the child will eventually need ongoing therapy (again, not free) from—can you guess?—yes! an adoption specialist! This therapy will help the adopted child come to grips (but never completely resolve) the problems that are inevitable to adoption—ongoing attachment issues, bonding problems, abandonment fears, grieving—which no good research has ever proven are inevitable to adoption.

Of course, when the child enters therapy, the parents will have to undergo separate therapy. Eventually, when the child is ready to tell his adoptive parents how he really feels about being adopted and their insufficiencies when it comes to helping him attach and bond, the entire family will have to endure very expensive family therapy. At some point, in order to help him resolve his "grieving," the child will be reunited with his biological mother (less often, his biological father), and they will go to Disney World together in order to forgive and rebond. And the child, now somewhere between the ages of eight and fourteen, will convince himself that if he lived with his "real" mother (or father), his life would be a bowl of cherries. At that point, he will become increasingly rebellious, withdrawn, sullen, passive-aggressive, disrespectful, and downright nasty in the home of his "fake" parents. As the home situation deteriorates, the adoptive parents will seek the counsel of their adoption specialist, who will recommend more therapy, this time including the biological parent or parents. And things will go steadily downhill from there. Someday, all these folks will be invited to appear on a daytime talk show, where much yelling and crying and accusations will take place, all to the entertainment of millions of couch potatoes who desperately need real lives of their own.

This is an example of what I call the adoption drama. I did not make up any of that description. It's a composite of horror stories related to me over the years by adoptive parents. One or more adoption specialists are always central to the drama. These people serve no purpose, it seems, other than to scare adoptive parents half to death, cause them constant anxiety and guilt, and lead them to believe that they need therapy from, yep, adoption specialists. These specialists were not needed fifty-plus years ago, when adoption was no big deal and adopted kids turned out fine (as the research says they still do, even without adoption specialists). It's become a big deal only because the livelihood of adoption specialists depends on convincing adoptive parents that it's a big deal, the single biggest parenting deal of them all.

The constant babble coming from most adoption specialists causes adoptive parents to obsess about the issue and lose sight of the fact that they are raising mere children. Instead, they come to believe they are raising a unique species, *Homo adoptus*. All of the professionally induced obsessing about the adjective, the modifier, causes them to almost forget the noun: child. As a result, they begin to see everything their children do through the distorting adoption filters that have been fitted to their parenting eyeballs. They begin to interpret their children's behavior according to the adoption mythology they've been force-fed by adoption babblers.

That's why adoptive parents almost always share the fact that their child is adopted within three sentences of beginning a conversation with me. Some real-life examples:

◆ "John, I wonder if I can talk to you about a problem I'm having with my six-year-old. He's started getting up in the middle of the night, and he wants to come into our bed. I guess I should tell you he's adopted."

◆ "My seven-year-old has recently developed a fear of thunder. This happened shortly after we were caught in a storm while driving to my parents' home in Virginia. I don't know if this is relevant, but we adopted her when she was three."

◆ "Our son is having social difficulties, mostly at school. He constantly complains of having no friends and that no one likes him, even though his teacher says she sees no problems at all. She says he gets along with the other kids just fine. We adopted him at birth, by the way. Do you think there might be a connection?"

The likelihood that the problems enumerated above have anything to do with the fact that these three real-life kids were adopted is slim to none. After all, there are nonadopted six-year-olds who for some strange reason suddenly want to sleep with their parents. And there are more nonadopted than adopted kids who are afraid of thunder. And lots of nonadopted kids complain of having no friends when the evidence proves otherwise. Self-drama is the stuff of childhood. These are nothing more than examples of the illogical, odd, strange things kids sometimes do—things that usually have no bearing whatsoever on how they were raised before the start of the illogical, odd, strange things in question.

But adoption babblers have convinced parents of adopted children that *anything* illogical, odd, or strange their children do is precisely *because* they were adopted. Behind every problem—emotional, social, academic, whatever—there's an adoption gremlin. Every little glitch—and all parents experience occasional glitches with their kids—screams "Adopted!" Everything out of the ordinary—and sooner or later, every child does things that are out of the ordinary—screams "Adopted!" Every imperfection, problem, misbehavior—all kids misbehave—screams "Adopted!"

Furthermore, the adoptive parent can't win for losing. If an adopted child is shy, it's because he was adopted! If an adopted child is very outgoing and occasionally violates other people's boundaries, it's because he was adopted! If an adopted child is irresponsible about schoolwork, it must be because he was adopted! If an adopted child is perfectionistic about schoolwork, it is probably because he was adopted! The adopted child is first and foremost *adopted*. Somewhere in there, if one searches hard and far enough, one will find a child.

Driving Parents Batty

I have the utmost respect and admiration for parents who adopt. I tell them they are cultural heroes. That's why I find it so disturbing and frustrating when I see so many of today's adoptive parents (especially mothers) experiencing unnecessary stress and anxiety. I'm referring here to the anxieties and fears manufactured by adoption specialists and the things they encourage adoptive parents to do: Keep up to date on the "latest findings" on the subject in an endless stream of articles and books by adoption "experts" who often write rubbish that has no good scientific underpinning, attend adoption support groups led by adoption specialists, and attend regular talks and seminars on adoption given and led by adoption specialists. Consequently, because the issue of adoption is constantly stirred and focused on to the point of near obsession, it begins to color the parents' perception of nearly everything the child does.

A perfect example of this is the mother of a three-year-old adopted boy who, she related, had started hugging everyone he met—other children as well as adults. She was certain these "inappropriate displays of affection" toward other people were indications that he had failed to properly bond with her. She was in a near panic.

When he was around three, my son Eric started hugging everyone he met. My wife and I thought it was cute, charming, adorable, and endearing. Other people did too. No one was put off by it. No one ever intimated that Eric's hugging constituted "inappropriate displays of affection." Furthermore, we were delighted that he felt such natural tenderness for other members of the human race. To us, it was indicative of the innocence and nonjudgmental nature of childhood. The idea that his hugging was improper never entered our minds. It's been forty years since Eric was a spontaneous people hugger, during which time I've heard of and seen lots of kids that same age hug people they've just met. Most of them were not adopted children. None of them were trying to resolve deep-seated psychological issues. They were simply affectionate.

Concerning little huggers, there will come a time when their parents should and will teach them that spontaneous hugging can make certain folks uncomfortable, and the hugging will become limited to close friends. Until then, I say adults should stand back and let these kids hug away. In other words, "spontaneous, persistent hugging behavior" (which is what a psychologist might call it) in a three-year-old is not out of the ordinary. It's certainly not an indication of something amiss—more specifically, that the hugger in question has failed to properly bond with his or her parents and is looking for someone, anyone, to bond with.

This adoptive mom's thinking had been contaminated by what I call "adoption boogeymen." In this case, the boogeymen took up residence in her mind during preadoption and postadoption counseling sessions with adoption specialists and as she read the adoption literature recommended by these same specialists. After the boogeymen were implanted in this mom's mind, they were fed by her attendance at meetings of her adoption support group, which consisted of other adoptive mothers and fathers whose ability to think straight about their children was similarly contaminated. These boogeymen scrabble around in the brains of adoptive parents, chattering and warning and making such a din that the parents are incapable of hearing the soft, calming voice of common sense coming from their hearts.

Lots and lots of adoptive parents have told me that adoption specialists warned them that from infancy, their children can sense they are not really their biological parents, but they don't know what to make of these strange feelings. Balderdash! The notion that children adopted during infancy or early to mid-toddlerhood—before the formation of permanent memory (see the Introduction)—somehow know that the people they're living with are not their biological parents and therefore grieve and develop these attachment problems is pure hokum. It would be laughable if not for the damage it causes to adoptive parents in the form of near-constant stress, anxiety, fear, self-doubt, and confusion.

Several years ago, I was conducting a seminar with a small group of parents, including a couple who had adopted a lovely daughter from China. At the time, the child was three years old. From day one, she had slept with her parents, and they wanted her out of their bed but were unsure about how to go about doing so, especially given that they'd been warned by their adoption specialist of the ever-looming risk of reactive attachment disorder (to be discussed later in this chapter). They were caught between the desire to reclaim their marital bed and anxiety about possible negative effects on their daughter.

I began talking about adoption myths and adoption boogeymen and the fact that most psychological diagnoses, including reactive attachment disorder, are not supported by good science, and I shared research to the effect that most adoption myths are simply wrong. The mother put her head down and began to weep, softly at first. I stopped talking as her crying quickly turned to chest-heaving sobs. Her husband put his arms around her and drew her close. She buried her face in his shoulder as her sobbing became louder and louder. I seriously wondered about the possibility that she would pass out from hyperventilating.

When she had wept herself out, she apologized to the group, which we all said was completely unnecessary. Then she tried to talk about her daughter, but she began to choke up again, so her husband took over. He told the group that they'd been informed by their adoption counselor that when Mom held her daughter to her breast, the little girl heard a heartbeat that was noticeably different from her biological mother's heartbeat, to which she had bonded in the womb. So she began to grieve for the loss of her biological mother. For three years, these parents had lived with constant fear that their daughter would never really accept them as her real parents (and by the way, his or her adoptive parents are an adopted child's *real* parents).

"This is the first time," he said, "that anyone with any authority has told us that this is malarkey." He went on to explain, as she nodded her head, that his wife was weeping with relief.

Indeed, the notion that an unborn child bonds to its mother's heartbeat and experiences psychological angst when it hears the heartbeat of its adoptive mother and begins to grieve as a result is pure, undiluted malarkey. It's crazy (the product of irrational thinking on the part of the person spreading such malarkey), and it's the sort of thing that makes adoptive parents crazy. Unfortunately, it's not unusual for adoption specialists and counselors to disseminate destructive adoption propaganda of this very destructive sort. In fact, I have found that it is the norm. In so doing, these "experts" cause adoptive parents to bring tremendous anxiety and insecurity to their parenting situation, thus making adoption specialists indispensable. The adoptive parents who are so infected, so anxious, so insecure become convinced they cannot find their way through the adoption minefield without the constant guidance of a person who represents the professional group that's planting the mines in the first place.

Adoption propaganda has caused many adoptive parents to be overly sensitive to any behavior that is even slightly outside some very narrow norm they constantly compare their kids to. Under the circumstances, they inevitably find what they are anxiously anticipating: behaviors that confirm that their kids are struggling with "adoption issues." Now beset with anxiety and insecurity, they respond to their kids' needs for guidance or discipline—needs inherent to the state of being a child, adopted or not—in less-than-effective ways. Sometimes, they even suggest to the kids that the problems they're having are adoption related. In either case, because these parents don't respond with loving authority to their children's problems, the problems are likely to continue. And the more the problems continue, the more anxious the parents become, and the less effectual their responses are, and the problems get worse. And 'round and 'round they all go. Psychologists refer to this as a self-fulfilling prophecy. Simply speaking, what one expects to find, one finds.

When I describe that self-perpetuating, downward-spiraling scenario to adoptive parents, they almost always can relate to it personally. This is the essence of the adoption drama I referred to earlier. To have someone who's not involved in the drama describe it is liberating to these parents. When they've taken these problems to adoption counselors, the counselors have confirmed their fears. Yes, a six-year-old who wakes up in the middle of the night and wants the comfort of his parents' bed is doing so because being alone in his own bed in a dark room stirs fears of abandonment. Under the circumstances, if the parents don't allow him in their bed, adoption-related problems will only fester and grow. He is likely to grow up to be an emotional basket case. As an adult, he is likely to compensate for his abandonment fears by seeking comfort in the arms of one woman after another. To stave off these possibilities, the parents need to let him into their bed, come to more counseling sessions, and put their son into play therapy, where he can act out his insecurities in a "safe place." To this and similar claims made by adoption counselors, my response is, "Hogwash!"

When Common Sense Ruled

When I was growing up, I knew a few adopted kids. Until they said they'd been adopted, there was no way anyone would have guessed. Nothing about them was out of the ordinary. They didn't hug other people spontaneously, for example. Besides, the average person didn't give the fact of a child's adoption a second thought, and adoptive parents didn't give it much thought either. There were practical issues involved, but they were purely practical. These included the question of when to inform the child of his adoption and how to best answer the inevitable questions: "Who were my biological parents? Why did they put me up for adoption? Where are my biological parents now?" These are questions every adopted child has every right to ask and to which he has every right to straightforward, honest answers. In some cases, the child might have been old enough at the time of adoption to remember his biological parents. In that event, the child would certainly have emotions that his parents would need to help him deal with. But no one felt the need to tiptoe around adopted kids because of the supposed ever-present threat that some inadvertent comment or behavior might trigger a latent adoption issue and throw the child into an emotional tailspin.

As a consequence of this very healthy attitude, adoption was not infused with drama, as it is today. The drama that swirls around adoption and adopted children today—involving the words *bonding, reactive attachment disorder, trust, adoption grief, abandonment,* and *anger*—has been manufactured by adoption professionals. There is no good scientific evidence that adopted children raised in loving families where no one makes the fact of adoption a big deal are any more prone to psychological problems than non-adopted kids. But there is plenty of anecdotal evidence that adoption mythology has been very destructive to lots of adoptive parents and has inhibited their ability to respond naturally to their children's needs, most importantly the need for firm discipline. This evidence is mostly in the form of first-person testimonies given by adoptive parents who have been able to recover from the propaganda and the brainwashing and finally think straight.

Apparently, it is not enough for adopted parents to simply love and properly discipline their children. They must be amateur therapists. If their children are to have any hope of a normal life, the parents must learn how to offset the psychological problems that are inherent to adoption.

Such a view almost inevitably leads to two equally unfortunate and unnecessary outcomes. First, it leaves many loving, well-intentioned moms and dads who desperately want nothing more than to love their children and devote themselves to being the best parents they can possibly be feeling anxious and guilty, obsessing over the possible long-term effects of even their smallest parental decisions. Second, it leads many parents to pay for professional "help" from so-called experts who propagate the same psychobabble that's feeding all their irrational fears and causing all their needless stress. A significant amount of the babble involves a disorder adopted children didn't have before the 1970s.

Reactive Attachment Babble

Most of the anxieties borne by adoptive parents center on the notion that any out-of-the-ordinary behavior on the part of an adopted child is evidence of a condition psychologists have dubbed reactive attachment disorder (RAD). In the 1950s, Dr. John Bowlby's research on Eastern European orphans led to the rise of attachment theory, the idea that children who are not afforded the opportunity to properly attach to a loving caregiver early in life are likely to suffer long-term, detrimental consequences. Many of Bowlby's conclusions make sense and come on the heels of thorough experimentation. Since I shared some details about Bowlby's research and the contributions he and some of his later disciples have made to child psychology in the earlier chapter on attachment, I will not rehash the same information here. Suffice it to say, attachment theory eventually led to the psychological diagnosis of RAD. This is a condition that arises in a person who fails to form secure, loving attachments to a primary caregiver at an early age due to neglect, abuse, separation, lack of stability, and so on.

According to the *Diagnostic and Statistical Manual of Mental Disorders (DSM)*, reactive attachment disorder is characterized by a "markedly disturbed and developmentally inappropriate social relatedness in most contexts" that cannot be accounted for solely by any developmental delay. In other words, kids with RAD interact with people in very strange and significantly inappropriate ways. It is important to note that the operative qualifier in the diagnosis is the phrase *markedly disturbed*. According to the best available evidence, the condition forms in infants and small children as a result of the children being denied the normal experiences necessary to form healthy attachment;

they've been abused or they've been bounced from caretaker to caretaker, none of whom has done more than provide basic needs.

Experts say that RAD typically manifests itself before age five. Children who are so diagnosed show a "persistent failure to initiate or respond in a developmentally appropriate fashion to most social interactions." They might even avoid social contact with people. As these kids grow, they show no empathy or concern for others. They often resist and even become upset by any attempt on the part of a caregiver to hold, nurture, or comfort them. Other RAD children might go in the opposite direction. Instead of withdrawing, these kids become indiscriminately sociable, frequently engaging in excessive displays of affection even toward total strangers. Mind you, these are not kids who are two or three years old. They are old enough and have the mental ability to know that spontaneous outbursts of affection make people uncomfortable. They simply don't pick up on social cues or feedback of that nature. Their need for close human contact takes over their lives.

Very definitely, some adopted children fit that description, but they are the rare exception, not the rule. Psychological studies and scientific experiments aside, common sense tells us that a child who is grossly neglected or abused over an extensive period early in life will be negatively affected by the experience. Surely one would expect such an ordeal to skew how a child views the world around him and his ability to trust and relate to people. I even agree that, for some of these children, trained professional help might be in order. But again, the tipping point involves the words "markedly disturbed." In and of itself, the fact that a three-year-old hides from unfamiliar people, won't look them in the eye or respond when spoken to, or becomes almost hysterical when his parents leave him with a sitter or at a nursery is not indication of the *marked disturbance* that characterizes RAD.

What is troubling when it comes to adoptive families isn't that the so-called experts and writers of adoption books and parenting articles draw attention to the possible effects of RAD. The problem is that they have unnecessarily poisoned the minds of adoptive parents with the unfounded notion that just about *any* adopted child—even those who do not come from abusive or grossly neglectful backgrounds—is prone to RAD.

Take, for instance, the parents of adopted toddler twin boys who suddenly began crying and reaching for their mother when she dropped them off at her church's nursery. She was elated because she had been led to believe (erroneously) that one sign of RAD is going easily to another caregiver (in this case, the person keeping the nursery). In this mom's mind, her twins' stress at seeing her leave was confirmation that they were adequately attached to her. That conclusion does not follow, of course, but this also means that if these twin boys had not shown distress at going to the church nursery, the mother would probably have been thrown into an anxiety-filled tizzy of self-doubt. In either case, the mother is misinterpreting her children's signals. Very simply, separation anxiety is not uncommon to young toddlers, adopted or not. My experience is that probably 99 percent of toddlers who suffer separation anxiety no longer suffer it by age four. And lack of separation anxiety in a young toddler, adopted or not, doesn't mean he has a better or worse mother than a child of the same age who suffers it. Why do some kids suffer it and some never do? Who knows? Why do some kids love spinach and some gag at the taste? Does the spinach-loving child have better parents?

Another example of specialist-induced adoption insanity is a real-life mother who was greatly distressed because her four-year-old adopted daughter had started telling everyone she met, including total strangers, details of the family's life that the parents would rather have remained private. Upon meeting someone, anyone, the child would say whatever was on her mind, as in, "My mommy and daddy argued this morning" or "Mommy's underpants are pink." The mother was completely freaked out. To her, the child's inability to keep family secrets meant that she wasn't sufficiently bonded. Her parents were just an interesting couple she lived with but had no emotional ties to. Over the course of my career, I've heard of many three- and four-year-old nonadopted children who have spontaneous blurting disorder. Take, for example, the four-year-old girl whose parents told her she could not stay up and watch a movie with them because it was a movie for adults. The next day in church, the little girl walked up to the minister and proudly announced that her parents watched adult movies.

I estimate that at least 90 percent of the behaviors adoptive parents attribute to adoption are nothing more than examples of the odd things kids sometimes do and say, and 90 percent may be a conservative estimate. In the 1950s and 1960s, a very popular television show called *Kids Say the Darndest Things* featured young kids saying odd and usually hilarious things while being interviewed by host Art Linkletter. I suppose some of the kids who appeared on the show were adopted, but I'm sure that most were not. They all blurted out family secrets. By the way, Art Linkletter had been adopted.

Those are but two of many examples of how all this babble about reactive attachment disorder has led to an epidemic of irrational fear among adoptive parents. Our culture has taken what is, according to the *DSM*, a rare condition and convinced adoptive parents that their kids are highly likely to suffer from it. Many adoptive parents have been led to believe that *all* adopted kids suffer from it to some degree and that the possibility of a megaeruption of attachment problems is an ever-present possibility. These parents believe their kids are sleeping RAD volcanoes that can blow at any minute.

The truth is that there's a good chance kids who were taken from their biological parents because of neglect or abuse and adopted by loving and responsible parents will end up okay. Even kids who are old enough to remember their biological parents and what life was like before adoption into a new family will probably end up okay, even without any therapy.

The Babble Begins

The first book to make adoption a significant issue was *Shared Fate: A Theory of Adoption and Mental Health,* by H. David Kirk. An adoptive father, Kirk directed the Adoption Research Project at McGill University from 1951 to 1961. This project eventually compiled data about the attitudes and experiences of two thousand adoptive families in Canada and the United States. Most of the parents in question had adopted because of infertility, a problem over which they had no control but which they felt was a social stigma. Kirk proposed that some of these couples compensated by denying that adoption was a qualitatively different family arrangement. For example, they did not think that it was important to talk to their children about their adoption or even tell them about it. They denied that they and their adopted children shared a common fate: They were different. On the other hand, adoptive parents who accepted this challenge had to work through some tough problems, but in the end both the parents and their adopted children would be better off for it. In other words, Kirk was proposing that adoption had potential therapeutic (healing) value for both parents and children.

Kirk's theory quickly became accepted wisdom in the adoption community, not because it was based on empirical evidence but because it was new and radical and fit the 1960s zeal for tossing out anything old. His writings were instrumental in promoting a 180-degree shift of adoption philosophy and practice away from matching adoptive parents with children who looked like them toward *diversity* of physical characteristics, even ethnicity, and away from confidentiality and sealed records toward open adoption.

Obviously, adoption is a *different* way to make a family. Kirk elevated this common-sense observation to a social theory. Bringing *difference* into the open made it important to know whether difference caused damage. Without empirical evidence, the mental health community began claiming that it did, that adoptees were unusually prone to behavior problems and emotional disturbance. Kirk actually protested this pessimistic conclusion, but his book had provided a platform for thinking about adoption as having latent emotional risks. In the blink of an eye, adoption was transformed from no big deal into a potentially apocalyptic undertaking. As a consequence, successful adoptive parents had to become quasi-therapists. Kirk said as much:

There is no doubt that adopters, along with other parents, seek to have families of stability and permanence, yielding personal satisfactions. Stability requires rules of conduct. Families that are not regulated by tradition must depend on the interpersonal skills of their members for their internal order. In the situation of adoption, these skills imply empathic and ideational communication with the child about his background.

Keep in mind that before the publication of *Shared Fate,* adoption was simply a way of creating or adding to a family and providing a home for children who might otherwise live in an orphanage. There were no risks, only benefits. Now there were risks, and risks required professionals who could help adoptive parents and adopted children successfully navigate the risks and deal with them if and when they reared their ugly little heads. The new specialists proliferated and spread the news of these supposed (unproven, then and now) risks, and adoptive parents became increasingly anxious. The more anxious they became about their ability to rise to the challenge (which had never been a challenge before), the more they turned to the new specialists for guidance. And the more the specialists babbled, the more anxious adoptive parents became. And that's how adoption pathology developed.

The Stone Rolls Downhill

In a 2010 article, adoption specialist Meghan Vivo claimed, "Many adopted and foster children have painful histories. . . . Between 50 percent and 80 percent of these children display symptoms of attachment disorder." Vivo's wording is very clever, disingenuous even. For one thing, displaying a symptom does not mean one has a disorder or disease. As I'm writing this, I am congested, a *symptom* of a sinus or other upper respiratory infection. However, I do not have an infection; I am suffering from my usual seasonal allergies. For another, the fact (if it is a fact) that a certain number of adopted children display symptoms of attachment disorder is meaningless without knowing how many symptoms they display, how often they display these symptoms, the specific symptoms in question, and the percentage of nonadopted children who also display the same symptoms. Conveniently, Vivo shares none of these vital statistics. She only creates the impression that adoption is a psychologically risky enterprise that requires continuing professional guidance.

On its Web site, the Mayo Clinic lists possible symptoms of RAD, separating them into symptoms in babies and symptoms in older children and teens. Most of the symptoms listed by Mayo are not found in the *Diagnostic and Statistical Manual* under *reactive attachment disorder.* Mayo is inflating the official symptom picture in a very unhelpful fashion. For example, Mayo claims that being "calm when left alone" is a possible RAD symptom in babies. So is "engaging in self-soothing behavior, such as rocking." The fact is that both of those supposed "symptoms" are sometimes exhibited by perfectly normal babies. Some babies, as soon as they're physically able to do so, discover the pleasure of getting up on their hands and knees and rocking back and forth, gently banging their heads against their crib headboards, to put themselves to sleep. In and of itself, this is not indicative of anything being wrong. In the vernacular of the profession, it is called *non-pathological head banging.*

Mayo's signs of attachment disorder in older kids and adolescents include "failing to ask for support or assistance," "awkwardness," and "masking feelings of anger." Again, perfectly normal teens act in those ways. Given Mayo's criteria, it is possible that 100 percent of infants, toddlers, and preschool-age, school-age, and teenage children "exhibit symptoms of attachment disorder"—*occasionally.*

It is widely recognized that RAD is one of the most poorly researched and least-defined disorders listed in the *DSM.* It is also widely acknowledged to be rare. In its latest incarnation, the *DSM* lists the following diagnostic criteria:

◆ Markedly disturbed and developmentally inappropriate social relatedness in most contexts.

◆ The disturbance is not accounted for solely by developmental delay.

◆ Onset before five years of age.

◆ A history of significant neglect.

◆ An implicit lack of an identifiable, preferred attachment figure.

Again, the RAD is a "marked" disturbance. To qualify for this rare disorder, a child must do more than simply exhibit a symptom or two here and there. One would not know any of this from reading Vivo's warning or Mayo's description. By failing to put her comments in proper context, Vivo creates the impression that RAD is rampant among adopted children. This simply is not true. The misinformation she and the Mayo Clinic dispense only causes adoptive parents to overinterpret any "odd" behavior on the part of their adopted kids.

Attachment Truth

Not all children who experience neglect, abuse, and instability are predestined to develop RAD or any other psychological disorder. Many experts acknowledge that good numbers of children who are denied normal attachment experiences as infants or small children will never develop an attachment disorder or be burdened by lingering adverse effects. Even kids who experience abrupt separation from or frequent change in caregivers early in life or who suffer severe neglect or abuse usually overcome their early experiences.

In what still stands as one of the defining scientific studies on the topic, renowned psychologist William Goldfarb conducted research in 1945 examining the effects of negative experiences and deprivation on institutionalized children. Goldfarb found that a large percentage of the children he studied were incredibly resilient.

They adjusted well, overcame the trauma of any early neglect, abuse, or instability in caregivers, and grew to be emotionally, mentally, and physically healthy individuals. More recent research shows that children who have suffered severe neglect or abuse and failed to bond with a primary caregiver at an early age can still form healthy attachments and social relationships later on. In short, there is very little evidence pointing to the inevitability of long-term problems for children who show early childhood behaviors associated with RAD.

In his book *The Myth of the First Three Years,* professor John Bruer debunks the notion that what children experience as infants and toddlers sets the course for how they will ultimately turn out:

There is also a substantial body of research that supports the claim that experiences throughout one's life have a profound effect on personality, character, and mental health and that these effects swamp the impact of early childhood experience.

Every parent who has adopted or is thinking of adoption should read Bruer's book. He relates findings pertaining to kids who were kept in Romania's horrifying orphanages before the Romanian people rose up and freed themselves from communist tyranny. These were kids whose caretakers rarely took them out of their cribs, much less held them; who changed their diapers no more than once a day; who dropped food into their cribs like they were caged animals; who didn't respond to their cries of distress. After being adopted into loving American families, many (but not all) recovered quite well. The research does find that early deprivation can be damaging, but it also finds that most of the damage can be reversed.

The bottom line: According to research, when it comes to healthy psychological development, there is absolutely no good, reliable evidence that adopted children, on the whole, have more strikes against them than any other child. Research has shown that not only do young adults who were adopted score similarly to their nonadopted counterparts on psychological tests, but those raised in stable homes by loving adoptive parents consistently score better than adults raised by biological parents who had been through a divorce, raised their kids as single parents, or raised their children in step-families.

In *Raising Adopted Children,* author Lois R. Melina cites research done at Rutgers and Yeshiva Universities in which adoptive parents and their adopted children were found to form attachments as successfully and often as biological families. Unlike many if not most adoption experts, Melina offers reassuring advice about attachment:

We [adoptive parents] don't need to be in a hurry to form attachment; we should enjoy the process, have fun with the child, and build up a reservoir of pleasant experiences.

Indeed!

The fact is that every child and teenager, adopted or not, is going to experience one or more of the following: anxiety, worry, sadness, fear, uncertainty, insecurity, questions, confusion, self-consciousness, and self-doubt. There is absolutely no evidence that nonadopted kids deal with these inevitabilities better than adopted kids, all other things being equal. One of the best studies of the long-term effect of adoption is ongoing in Sweden, where researchers have concluded that adoptees, as adults, are no more at risk for adverse outcomes than any other group of people in the general population.

All of this should cause a collective sigh of relief among adoptive parents. If actual scientific data are any indication, it turns out that their love and devotion to their children will do far more to define the outcome of the children's lives than any negative experiences the children may have endured early on. For the overwhelming majority of kids who have experienced early trauma, loving parents are all they need.

Even kids who come to loving adoptive parents from abusive and neglectful backgrounds stand a very good chance—much better than 50–50—of turning out just fine. All adoptive parents have to do is love them and give them time. They don't have to let them sleep in the marital bed, sing lullabies with adoption themes, constantly ask their kids to express their feelings about having been adopted, or otherwise walk on eggshells. To paraphrase the refrain of a Buck Owens song the Beatles covered early in their career, "All they gotta do is act naturally."

Acting Naturally

I have a friend who at age nineteen was at a family reunion with his parents and several dozen relatives. He walked up to a group of relatives who were talking, and one of them turned and said, "Hey there, Larry! We're talking about adoption. You were adopted, so why don't you jump in?"

He made some excuse, found his parents, got them off to one side, and asked, "Uncle Jack says I was adopted. Was I?"

His father said, "Yes, Larry, you were."

Astonished, Larry asked, "Why didn't you tell me?"

To which his father replied, "What difference would that have made?"

He thought about that and said, "You're right. None."

And that was pretty much that. His parents said they planned on telling him when he was about to be married. Actually, there wasn't much to tell. A young woman had Larry out of wedlock. His parents happened to find out about the young woman's situation and approached her with the offer to adopt her child. She was grateful, Larry's father and mother were grateful, and Larry was certainly grateful that he had grown up with advantages he might not have had, in a home where both parents were present.

As of this writing, Larry is sixty years old. He's intelligent, personable, funny, well liked, gracious, responsible, and compassionate. He's a man of good moral and ethical character. He told me this story because I told him I was writing this book. Until then, I had no idea he was adopted.

The point is that his parents, to their credit, felt that the fact of his adoption was not some psychological loaded gun in Larry's life. They didn't think it was a big deal, so they never told him about it. By the way, I am not implying that adopted children should not be told they were adopted. Before the advent of adoption specialists and adoption babble, the child was usually told he or she was adopted somewhere between age eight and eighteen, depending on circumstances. I know plenty of adopted adults who were informed at some time between those birthdays. None of them complain about it.

But Larry's parents adopted him sixty years ago, before adoption specialists and therefore before adoption babble. No one ever lent drama to the circumstances of his life. His parents didn't spend much of his childhood worrying about him, seeing adoption gremlins behind every glitch in his behavior.

That may be the very reason he's such a well-adjusted guy.

Spanking Babble

*"If you tell a lie big enough and keep repeating it,
people will eventually come to believe it."*

—Joseph Goebbels

I was a guest on *The View* once. Barbara Walters began the discussion by saying, "John, I understand you believe in spanking." She just let the statement hang there.

I said, "No, I do not." She looked panicked, for good reason. She was confident I would admit to being a mean-spirited right-wing Neanderthal posing as a parenting expert and had planned the interview accordingly. I'd upset her plans, and she didn't know what to say. So I rescued her: "The idea that one *believes* in spanking makes it sound like religious doctrine. No, I don't *believe* in it, but I think it's an appropriate response to some misbehavior, with some children, sometimes." Relief flooded Barbara's face. And the discussion proceeded from there to nowhere, which is where such talk show discussions usually go.

The subject of spanking is a sticky wicket indeed. It has definitely generated more attention than it merits. In fact, it seems there's an unhealthy fascination with the topic, as if whether one is for spankings or against them is all one needs to know about a person.

One reason I rarely open the floor to questions at a speaking engagement is because of the risk someone will ask, "Do you believe in spanking?" At that point, no matter which direction I step, I step in "it." Some people will be upset if I appear to be endorsing corporal punishment. Others will be upset if I seem opposed to it. Making matters worse is that people who are adamantly opposed to whacking children on their rear ends seem to think that if a person isn't against spanking, he must be for it. It's a black-or-white issue to them. Maybe I'm kidding myself, but I take a middle ground on the subject. I'm neither for spankings nor against them. Here's what I think:

◆ Parents should exercise the option to spank very conservatively, if for no other reason than that the more a child is spanked, the less effective (if they ever were) the spankings become.

◆ Most parents spank badly, so the spankings accomplish nothing and may even make matters worse.

◆ Some children respond well to spankings; others do not.

◆ A child who does not respond well to spankings won't respond well to harder or more frequent spankings either.

◆ Spankings per se do not constitute abuse, but a spanking can be administered abusively, as can any other punitive consequence.

◆ A careful reading of the Bible does not compel the conclusion that God wants parents to spank misbehaving children with "rods" of one sort or another.

I have never specifically recommended that parents spank a child. I will not make such a recommendation simply because I have no way of knowing whether the parent in question will spank properly or the child in question will respond positively. It is my intention, always, to teach parents that effective discipline is conveyed not primarily by methods, spanking or otherwise, but through effective communication of instructions and expectations. Unfortunately, most parents who spank have failed to do just that.

Feelings, Nothing More Than Feelings

In 1979, I wrote a newspaper column in which I said that existing research did not support a notion the mental health community was then rallying around: that spankings per se did psychological harm to children. At the time, I was writing a weekly column for *The Charlotte Observer* and a number of other newspapers and serving as director of early intervention services at Charlotte's community mental health center.

The day after the column appeared in print, I was summoned to a meeting with my boss, also a psychologist. He informed me that numerous concerned citizens had complained to him about what I'd written and that, in his estimation, I was advocating child abuse. I pointed out to him that no impartial researcher had found that children who were occasionally spanked showed long-term ill effects. That didn't matter, he said. The long and short of it was that the only pertinent opinion was his, and he did not approve of spanking, and that was that. He wanted to begin "supervising" my column, which I'd been writing before I came to work at the center. I told him I couldn't allow that, as it amounted to censorship. He wasn't at all happy with my rejection of his generous offer. Reading the handwriting on the wall, I promptly got my ducks in a row and resigned a few months later.

That was my first experience with the irrationality that the topic of spanking evokes in people. Otherwise intelligent, well-educated people let their feelings rule their thinking when it comes to the subject, to the profound detriment of their ability to think straight. As a result, spanking occupies a place of prominence in America's parenting discourse that it does not merit. The typical arguments, pro and con, are often nothing short of dumb. One reason for this is the highly visible presence of extremists on both sides of the issue.

On the extreme left are people who believe that a swat to a child's rear end constitutes child abuse and that if parents won't voluntarily stop spanking, the government should make them stop. They justify government intrusion into family matters because they believe the end justifies the means.

The fact is that more than three decades after that strained confrontation with my boss at the Charlotte–Mecklenburg Mental Health Center, nothing has changed. Good research done by objective people who are seeking the truth and not trying to advance a political agenda (the operative qualifiers) does not support the notion that spankings per se put children at risk of later emotional or behavioral problems. More than thirty years later, good research finds that kids who are moderately (as opposed to brutally or abusively) spanked on occasion (as opposed to frequently) by parents who love them unconditionally have fewer emotional and social problems than kids who've never been spanked. Thirty-plus years later, that still doesn't matter to people who want the government to stop parents from spanking. All that matters is how they *feel*, which includes their obvious desire to win this debate by any means necessary.

On the extreme right are people who believe that God himself has enjoined parents to spank misbehaving children with "rods" of various sorts—belts, paddles, switches, wooden spoons, and the like. It doesn't matter to these folks that most Old Testament scholars do not believe that God has ordered anything of the sort. They read that "the rod of discipline" will drive foolishness from a child's heart (Proverbs 22:15), and nothing short of God himself could persuade them that the word *rod,* in that context, does not refer to a hard or flexible object. In fact, the people in question sometimes regard a fellow believer who challenges that view as a heretic of sorts.

Concerning spanking, here is the proper biblical context: What Christians call the Old Testament is the *only* testament for Jewish people. The books of that canon were written down by Jews, beginning with Moses. Do Jewish scholars believe God has commanded parents to beat children with hard or flexible objects when they misbehave? No, they do not. Do they think God has commanded parents to spank at all, even with their hands? Again, they do not. No specific form of punitive discipline is mentioned in the Old Testament. That should be the end of the discussion. On this subject, Christian parenting experts should defer to the opinion—the legitimate authority—of respected Hebrew scholars.

My experience has been that the extremists on the left will not moderate their views, no matter what evidence one puts in front of them. They are zealots, determined to see their views transformed into coercive law. I have found it impossible to reason with them.

That has not been as much the case with folks on the Christian right, however. Over the years, I've seen more and more willingness on their part to accept a softened position regarding spanking, one that is more in keeping with proper biblical exegesis. I will explain that position later in this chapter. Nonetheless, the notion that "the rod" of scripture is not a literal object is dying hard in some Christian circles.

My hope in this chapter is to help the reader put this issue into proper perspective, with the additional hope that a proper perspective will translate to more effective parenting behavior.

Meet Murray Straus, Anti-Spanker-in-Chief

Dr. Murray Straus is the founder and codirector of the Family Research Laboratory at the University of New Hampshire. He has produced most of the research used by antispanking groups to bolster their argument that spankings constitute child abuse and put children at later risk of emotional and social problems, including the increased risk of later criminality. Mind you, Straus's research does not *prove* any of this.

Unfortunately, Straus long ago crossed the line between science and advocacy. I believe it is accurate to say that he is a social activist first and a scientist second. Some time ago, he aligned himself with international antispanking groups such as End Physical Punishment of Children (EPOCH) and he has since become the equivalent of their patron saint. People from EPOCH and the Center for Effective Discipline and other like-minded organizations invoke his name more than anyone else's. Make no mistake, however: Straus truly believes what he says about spanking. I think he believes it so ardently that he has no problem making sure his research finds what he already believes to be true.

Straus claims to have found conclusive evidence that kids who are spanked are more likely than nonspanked kids to have emotional and adjustment problems of all sorts and grow up to become wife beaters, criminals, and other deviant types. But Straus's evidence can't be considered conclusive for the simple reason that other researchers have failed to come up with similar data.

The Other Side of the Story

Robert Larzelere is a professor and research methodologist in the College of Human Sciences at the University of Oklahoma. His primary area of specialty is research into parental discipline—more specifically, parental spanking. Over the course of his largely academic career, Larzelere has faithfully used the scientific method to determine what disciplinary methods get the best results at what ages. As of this writing, he has authored or coauthored thirty-nine published papers on discipline, most of which concern spanking in one way or another, and has presented at numerous professional meetings. He is an academician in the purest sense of the term. Unlike his former mentor, Straus, he has no dog in the race, as we southerners put it; he has not aligned himself with any group of political activists. Bob Larzelere's cause, his purpose, is simply to discover the truth.

After obtaining his PhD in human development and family studies from Pennsylvania State University, Larzelere spent a postdoctoral year being trained in family research methods by none other than Murray Straus. When Straus published data showing that spanking was associated with greater risk for later antisocial behavior. Suspicious of Straus's conclusions, Larzelere analyzed his design and found that his data did not lead to any firm conclusions about spanking, one way or the other. He went public with his findings, and Straus responded by publicly castigating him in the introduction to his book *Beating the Devil Out of Them* (Lexington Books, 1994).

In 2010, Larzelere worked separately with two research teams, analyzing Straus's data. In both cases, he came to the conclusion that Straus's research design, when applied to nonphysical forms of punishment, produced similar data and led to the same conclusion. When Straus's research design is applied to time-out, for example, it "proves" that time-out produces later antisocial behavior. It's difficult to believe that Straus doesn't know his design is biased toward negative outcomes.

According to Larzelere, Straus has consistently refused to accept that his research method invites legitimate criticism. Whenever another researcher shows his evidence to be faulty or finds evidence to the contrary, Straus dismisses the critique, preferring to believe that anyone who disagrees with him is ill informed or biased.

Research conducted by Larzelere and others finds that when administered by parents who love their children unconditionally, who are generally affectionate toward them, and who take the time to explain themselves to their kids, moderate spankings (one or two swats with an open, empty hand) are not associated with any negative outcome; quite the contrary, in fact. When spankings conform to this definition and take place in the aforementioned conditions, they are associated with *better* behavior and *better* overall adjustment. Larzelere has also discovered that mild spankings increase the effectiveness of other disciplinary methods such as time-out and taking away privileges. Mind you, Larzelere does not *recommend* spanking; he is by no means asserting that spankings are *necessary* to growing a well-behaved, well-adjusted child. He is simply reporting conclusions he has developed in the process of dispassionate investigation.

Larzelere and I share serious concern about the effects, both intended and unintended, of government regulations on spanking. In 1979, Sweden became the first country to ban physical punishment of children. Ten years later, Larzelere found that child abuse had actually increased in Sweden since the ban. This finding is consistent with research psychologist Diana Baumrind's finding that parents who do not believe in spanking often report in private interviews that they have exploded toward their children in emotionally and sometimes physically abusive rages. Baumrind concludes that the occasional spanking serves as a safety valve of sorts, venting off parental emotions that might otherwise build up to explosive, even abusive intensity.

Other researchers have also confirmed Larzelere's findings about the ultimate deleterious effects of antispanking legislation. A 2009 study published in the *Akron Law Review* found that children raised in Sweden since the ban on spanking went into effect were more likely, as older teens and young adults, to be involved in crime, including violent crime, than children raised in countries where no such ban existed.

The lead researcher, professor Jason M. Fuller of the University of Akron Law School, found that Swedish teen violence skyrocketed in the early 1990s among children who had grown up after the ban took effect. Fuller noted, "By 1994, the number of youth criminal assaults had increased by six times the 1984 rate." An increase of this size could result from other factors, but a sixfold increase in ten years, during which time Swedish parents' hands were tied when it came to discipline, can certainly be attributed to Sweden's spanking ban.

Fuller also discovered that since the spanking ban and an extensive government-run parent education campaign, child abuse rates in Sweden have increased more than 500 percent. He reported that "not only were Swedish parents resorting to pushing, grabbing, and shoving more than U.S. parents, but they were also beating their children twice as often," and "from 1979 to 1994, Swedish children under seven endured an almost six-fold increase in physical abuse."

Evidence contrary to Straus's conclusions continues to mount. In January 2010, research psychologist Marjorie Gunnoe reported findings from her study of 179 teenagers who had been spanked as children. Gunnoe concluded, "The claims made for not spanking children fail to hold up. They are not consistent with the data."

In Gunnoe's study, teenagers who had been spanked as children scored higher than nonspanked teens in a number of critical areas. Among other things, they performed better in school, their outlook on life was more optimistic, and they were more willing to perform volunteer work. On no measure of adjustment, achievement, or morality did nonspanked kids score higher than those who had been spanked.

Gunnoe's 2010 report was largely ignored by the mainstream media in the United States. However, that was not the first time that her research had been overlooked. Her 1997 report showing that moderate spankings were associated with reduced aggression also received scant media attention. Meanwhile, the same media continue to make headlines out of Straus's questionable conclusion that spanking is associated with later aggression and criminality. Drama sells.

If Gunnoe's study stood alone in the field, serious questions could be raised as to its validity, but it does not. After tracking the children of 164 families from ages four to fourteen, psychologist Diana Baumrind found "no evidence for unique detrimental effects of normative physical punishment" and concluded that spanking can be helpful in certain disciplinary situations. She also found that children who were never spanked tended to exhibit more behavior problems than spanked children.

The most recent salvo in the spanking wars was fired off by Robert Larzelere and Diana Baumrind in a 2010 paper titled "Are Spanking Injunctions Scientifically Supported?" In this eighty-seven-page monograph, they meticulously review the research and come to several pertinent conclusions, among which are the following:

◆ "Multiple studies have shown that spanking is associated with adverse outcomes only when children perceive their parents as rejecting them." In other words, adverse outcomes are not predictable from spanking itself but occur when spanking parents are verbally hostile (screaming, cursing, belittling) and psychologically controlling (manipulative withdrawal of love). All of the most effective parents—those whose kids scored highest on measures of adjustment—spanked. In fact, they spanked as often, on average, as the parents whose kids scored lowest. Obviously, the effectiveness of spankings is a matter of the context in which they occur.

◆ "Even the most clinically defiant two- to six-year-olds will cooperate with time-out if enforced when necessary with an effective back-up tactic, such as a two-swat spank or room isolation." Eventually, say the authors, authoritative parents can phase out the backup consequence as children learn to cooperate with time-out and firm verbal correction. Larzelere and Baumrind suggest that when parents do not have the option to spank, they are likely to respond to defiance with permissiveness, verbal hostility, or occasional abusive rages. That hypothesis is consistent with follow-up findings concerning Sweden's spanking ban.

It is safe to say that the preponderance of research data collected by unbiased people—including Larzelere, Baumrind, Gunnoe, and Fuller—makes perfectly clear that spanking per se is not harmful, that children who are *never* spanked are at higher risk of all manner of adjustment difficulties, and that antispanking laws have not served the best interests of children. Has the evidence persuaded anyone in the antispanking movement to change sides? No. Among antispanking zealots, feelings continue to prevail:

◆ Since Sweden made the mistake of banning parental spanking, dozens of countries—including Germany, Italy, and New Zealand—have followed Sweden's foolhardy lead. In New Zealand, using physical force to discipline children is a felony involving full criminal penalties, and a parent cannot even legally take a child's hand to move him when he does not want to be moved. It appears that other countries think the results of Sweden's antispanking ban are anomalous.

◆ The United Nations Committee on the Rights of the Child continues to challenge laws permitting physical punishment of children. The committee calls on all governments in the world to sign and obey the articles of the United Nations Convention on the Rights of the Child, an international treaty that obligates signatory nations to prohibit every form of physical discipline.

◆ In the United States, the National Association of Social Workers has published a policy statement declaring that all physical punishment of children is harmful and should be outlawed. In my estimation, it is unethical for an influential professional body to publish a policy statement that ignores contrary evidence.

◆ In 2007, San Francisco Bay area assemblywoman Sally Lieber proposed legislation imposing a California state ban on spanking children under the age of three, punishable by a fine or jail time. "I think it's pretty hard to argue you need to beat a child three years old or younger," said Lieber. I agree with that. In fact, I'll expand that to include any age child. But of course Lieber is using *beat* to mean any swat to a child's rear parts, and in so doing she is revealing a predilection for emotional hyperactivity, the province of the demagogue.

◆ On DrSpock.com, a Web site devoted to continuing the work of pediatrician and author Benjamin Spock, one learns that "Spanking teaches children that the larger, stronger person has the power to get his way, whether or not he is in the right" and "The American tradition of spanking may be one reason that there is much more violence in our country than in any other comparable nation." In the first edition (1946) of his groundbreaking *Common-Sense Book of Baby and Child Care*, Dr. Spock took a thoughtful, moderate stance on spanking, saying that he wasn't specifically recommending it, but he felt it was preferable to "a long-winded [parental] diatribe." It is nothing short of naive to blame societal violence on spanking.

◆ The American Academy of Pediatrics' official policy on spanking states that "spanking is a less effective strategy than time-out or removal of privileges for reducing undesired behavior in children." This simply is not true. Some children don't respond to spankings; some don't respond to anything but. There is no single rule. Repeated attempts by Robert Larzelere, Diana Baumrind, and other credible researchers to properly educate the academy have fallen on deaf ears.

The move toward equating spanking and child abuse has been accelerating in recent years. In 2011, George W. Holden, representing the Society for Research in Human Development (SRHD), a supposedly unbiased academic body, proposed that the SRHD support "banning and eliminating corporal punishment of children in homes, schools, and all locations." The document is full of polemic, half-truths, distortions, and downright untruths. For example, Holden asserts, "CP [corporal punishment] has not been found by researchers to result in any positive outcomes except for immediate compliance." As we have seen, that simply isn't true. Holden should know of research done by Larzelere, Baumrind, and Gunnoe, all of whom have found distinct positive outcomes associated with spanking. Is he implying these folks don't have valid research credentials?

In his SRHD proposal, Holden says spanking is "outdated, ineffective, and violent." In response, I will assert the following:

◆ If longevity is one of the criteria by which a disciplinary method should be judged inappropriate, then that would include temporary restrictions on a child's mobility and a stern lecture.

◆ No discipline method is completely effective, but several credible researchers have demonstrated that spanking is by no means ineffective.

◆ Without exception, when I ask an adult whether he or she thinks spankings received as a child constituted "violence," the answer has been an unqualified "no." I will admit that my informal poll is not scientific. I will also concede that there undoubtedly are people who would answer in the affirmative. Nonetheless, my limited data are sufficient to nullify Holden's assertion.

Holden goes on to say that spanking "does not promote positive, warm, and respectful relationships in schools or families." Funny—I know plenty of parents who spank who appear to have very positive relationships with their kids, and the kids respect them. On the basis of these blatant falsehoods, Holden proposes that spanking be banned by the government.

This is very different from saying that parents should be counseled to replace spanking with alternative methods of discipline. Obviously, Holden thinks little of the average parent and a lot of himself by comparison. In his view, parents who spank are not educable; they're just too ignorant and stubborn to be persuaded, even by his superior intellect and wisdom. Because they won't voluntarily stop spanking, the government should force them to stop. Holden's attitude, shared by many, is a threat to the constitutional foundations of individual freedom.

Robert Larzelere respectfully asked Holden to consider engaging in constructive dialogue about the evidence, pro and con. Holden replied that the ethical issues remain the same regardless of evidence contrary to his position. In other words, spanking is unethical no matter the facts. Why? Because he, Holden, thinks it is.

Larzelere writes, "I do not doubt the good intentions of anyone supporting spanking bans. But without reasonably conclusive scientific evidence, my question is this: When is it ethical for one group to impose a set of absolutist values on others by law rather than by persuasion?"

I disagree with Larzelere on this point. My question is this: How can someone who wants to impose their arguable opinion on the general public by force of law be legitimately regarded as good intentioned? I, for one, do not give people like George Holden the benefit of the doubt. Call it mean-spirited if you like, but I believe people like him are pragmatists who believe in their moral superiority.

Their word on a subject is the final word; therefore, the end justifies their means.

And Now, from the Right

A majority of evangelical Christians, for reasons having primarily to do with their tendency to hold to the literal, contemporary meaning of words that appear in the Bible, believe that God has commanded parents to spank misbehaving children with various forms of "the rod" referred to primarily in the Book of Proverbs. The two most well known of these verses are as follows:

◆ "Those who spare the rod of discipline hate their children. Those who love their children care enough to discipline them" (Proverbs 13:24, New Living Translation).

◆ "Folly is bound up in the heart of a child, but the rod of discipline shall drive it far from him" (Proverbs 22:15, New International Version).

For nearly two decades, I have been publicly saying that the biblical word *rod,* when used in reference to the discipline of children, is not a rigid or flexible object such as a switch, belt, paddle, or wooden spoon. The misunderstanding arises because (a) this has been the traditional interpretation in the Christian community, and (b) proper rules of biblical exegesis (interpretation) are not being employed.

Concerning the latter, the standard rule of biblical interpretation is that scripture interprets scripture. This means that in attempting to understand any biblical word, phrase, or verse, one should look for consistencies in its use across the entirety of scripture. Using that rule, one finds that the word *rod* is used in two ways in the Bible: "a rod" and "the rod." The article—*a* or *the*—makes all the difference.

When the reference is to "*a* rod," the rod in question is clearly an object—a stick, a staff, a ruler's scepter. These objects are used, respectively, to measure length or strike someone, to herd, and to symbolize authority. And yes, "a rod" can also be a stick used to hit someone.

When the reference is to "*the* rod," however, the usage is clearly metaphorical. For example, in Isaiah 11:4, one reads that God "shall smite the earth with the rod of his mouth." In Lamentations 3:1, the reference is to "the rod" of God's wrath. No biblical scholar believes that an actual rod projects from God's mouth, nor do any biblical scholars believe God expresses his anger with a literal rod. In both cases, "*the* rod" is a powerful metaphor for God's supreme authority.

In every instance, when the word *rod* is used in the context of disciplining children, it is used as "the rod." Therefore, in keeping with the "scripture interprets scripture" rule, *the rod* in this usage is metaphorical. Dictionary.com defines *metaphor* as "a figure of speech in which a word or phrase is applied to something to which it is not literally applicable, in order to suggest a resemblance." In other words, writers use metaphors symbolically, to draw economical comparisons that more effectively communicate their meaning. In keeping with the word's use in other contexts, then, "the rod of discipline" is a reference to firm, consistent, parental authority. It is important to note that "the rod of discipline" is associated not with parental anger but with parental love, as in Proverbs 13:24.

This belies the repeated assertion, put forth by numerous Christian parenting authors, that God has prescribed spankings with rodlike objects when children misbehave. Why, God has not prescribed spankings at all, even with a parent's hand! The Bible, regarded as God's word, prescribes firm, consistent parental leadership until the child in question is capable, by example, correction, and training, of making good decisions on his or her own behalf.

The final nail in the coffin of this misunderstanding is found by comparing two biblical passages:

◆ Proverbs 23:13: "Do not withhold discipline from your child. If you punish him with the rod, he will not die."

◆ Exodus 21:20: "If a man strikes his male or female slave with a rod and he dies at his hand, he shall be punished."

One is moved to ask, "If 'the rod' and 'a rod' are the same, if they are both actual objects, then how is it that beating a strong adult male with "a" rod may result in his death, but beating a much weaker and more vulnerable child with "the" rod will not result in his death? The only way to resolve this seeming contradiction is to understand that "a rod" and "the rod" are not one and the same. A rod is a potentially lethal object. The rod is not lethal, by any stretch; it is a metaphor.

I need to point out that spankings, no matter how frequent, are by no means essential to raising a well-behaved child. Lots of never-spanked kids are well behaved and well adjusted. The statistics cited here do not mean otherwise. They simply mean that on average, kids who are spanked score higher than nonspanked kids on measures of adjustment. But there are exceptions to that general finding in both categories: There are nonspanked kids who are very polite and well behaved and spanked kids who are rude, disrespectful, disobedient, and generally out of control.

What is not arguable is that proper parental authority, conveyed according to known leadership principles, is as essential to the proper upbringing of a child as unconditional love.

If You're Going to Spank

As I said at the start of this chapter, I refuse to recommend spanking to any parent concerning any offense committed by a child because I have no way of knowing how the child will react to the spanking and I cannot be sure that the parent will spank properly. Some children react negatively to spankings; in other words, spankings worsen their behavior. And my experience has led me to conclude that most parents do not spank properly. Furthermore, I do not believe spankings are an essential ingredient of effective authoritative parenting.

But I don't *disapprove* of them either. I think spankings have their useful place. When pressed to make specific recommendations about their use, I rely primarily on the excellent, unbiased research done by Robert Larzelere and Diana Baumrind.

Remember that Baumrind identifies three types of parents (see chapter two): authoritarian, authoritative, and permissive. Interestingly enough, the authoritative parents in her study group spanked as much as authoritarian parents but obtained the best parenting outcomes. In fact, *all* of the authoritative parents spanked, prompting Baumrind to propose that authoritative parenting may require the occasional spanking. Of the three groups, their kids scored highest on various indices of adjustment. Authoritarian parents obtained the worst outcomes. Permissive parents came in second but well behind the authoritative parents.

In their 2010 article, Baumrind and Larzelere refer to "a normative spanking" as one or two swats to a child's rear end administered with the parent's open, empty hand. That is sufficient to get the message across. It's important to note that the effectiveness of a spanking does not increase with its severity. The point of diminishing returns is reached early on, around two swats. I think it's okay, especially with kids five and older, to go to four swats, but no more. The tendency of authoritarian parents to administer severe, even clearly abusive spankings may go a long way toward explaining why they are the most likely group to obtain negative long-term outcomes.

Larzelere and Baumrind do not recommend spanking a child before his or her second birthday, although they admit there may be some advantage to an occasional spank between eighteen and twenty-four months. And they find that spankings beyond the sixth birthday are generally ineffective. I don't have a problem with them up to age eight, but if parents have not effectively established their authority by then, spankings definitely are not the answer.

Spankings are most effective, say Baumrind and Larzelere, when they are used as an "enhancer" to other disciplinary methods such as time-out, removal of privilege, or in-room isolation. In my experience, however, time-out is not a generally effective consequence, especially with highly defiant children. It works with children who are already fairly well behaved. The exception is two-year-olds, for whom I recommend a five- to ten-minute time-out period (if the child will stay that long). After the third birthday, I generally recommend several hours of in-room isolation along with removal of privilege for several days to a week to drive the message home.

A spanking is justified (but not necessary) in response to belligerent defiance toward a parent or teacher, physical aggression toward a parent, belligerent verbal disrespect toward a parent or other adult, lying (as opposed to simply making up fanciful stories that aren't true), stealing, cursing, hitting a younger sibling, and making fun of someone who is handicapped. I deal in much greater depth with these and other misbehaviors in my book *The Well-Behaved Child* (Thomas Nelson, 2009).

After a spanking, the parent should remain with the child until crying stops, after which the parent should reassure the child of his love. I don't think one needs to make a big deal of this, however. Forgiveness is the more important thing. In other words, after the spanking and the follow-up punishment have been served, the parent forgives—making it clear that forgiveness does not imply permission to repeat the misbehavior—and the child's behavior slate is wiped clean.

At some point, either before or after a spanking, depending on which is more practical, the parent should take time to clearly, without anger, explain to the child why the spanking was administered, also making clear that the misbehavior in question will not be tolerated, ever, under any circumstances.

That brings us to the oft-heard admonition to never spank in anger. I agree with that, but I think that a spanked child should hear a clear message of disapproval from the parent. So never spank in anger, but never administer a spanking without some force of emotion behind it either.

And remember, if you don't want to spank, don't. That's okay too. It's by no means essential to growing a responsible adult.

CHAPTER
NINE

The Beat Goes On

"The devil can cite Scripture for his purpose."

—SHAKESPEARE (*THE MERCHANT OF VENICE*)

As I was writing this book, I was traveling the length and breadth of the United States giving talks mostly to parent groups. As is usually the case, a good number of parents told me of encounters with therapists that cost them significant amounts of money and resulted in no gain. Some of these encounters seemed to make matters worse. They told me of therapists (including psychologists, clinical social workers, marriage and family therapists, and family counselors) who talked to their children about behavior problems and feelings. There is no good evidence that when a child's behavior is drastically amiss, having a stranger talk to him will move things off square one. In fact, it can make things worse.

Parents also told me about therapists who talked to them about their children's lack of self-esteem as if they were completely ignorant of research findings that disavow the value of high self-esteem. They told me of therapists recommending that they be less "dictatorial," that they be more willing to negotiate and compromise with their children, as if the exercise of firm parent authority is a problem and not a solution to a problem.

They told me of therapists who told them—without evidence from any physical tests—that their children had inherited genes that caused biochemical imbalances. That's called practicing medicine without a license. Actually, claiming to know someone's biology without doing any physical tests is more accurately called lying.

They told me of therapists recommending behavior modification strategies that didn't work and then being told by these same therapists that these manipulations weren't working because they, the parents, weren't being consistent enough. As I said in the Introduction, no one has ever proven what B. F. Skinner himself failed to prove: the proposition that behavior modification works on human beings.

They told me of therapists recommending play therapy for children who were out of control at home. No controlled study done by an unbiased person has ever verified the efficacy of play therapy.

They told me of therapists claiming they had to give expensive batteries of tests in order to determine whether their kids had attention deficit–hyperactivity disorder. Not one of the criteria for this disorder listed in the *Diagnostic and Statistical Manual* is based on test results.

These stories go on and on. I conclude that many mental health professionals have severe cases of parent-babble disorder.

In 2011, Keith Ablow, a psychiatrist and member of the Fox News Medical A-Team, published *Inside the Mind of Casey Anthony* (St. Martin's Press). The subject of the title was a Florida mother accused of murdering her two-year-old daughter, Caylee. The mother's trial was a major news story for weeks. The jury returned a verdict of not guilty, but many people continue to think justice was not served.

In his book, Ablow proposes that the makings of Caylee Anthony's death go back five generations, to great-grandparents who were abandoned by their parents, never trusted men, and had a daughter (Casey's mother) who was the youngest of five siblings and the only girl. Her brothers resented her, and she became controlling toward men, a skill she perfected with the man she married, Casey's ineffectual father. This very controlling and self-absorbed mother ignored Casey's "personhood," and Casey in turn ignored Caylee. Whether Casey was directly responsible for Caylee's death, she was at least somewhat responsible, but so are her parents, grandparents, and great-grandparents. Or something like that. Ablow can prove none of this, of course. He's pulling his theories out of thin air. He has filled 256 pages with what in my estimation qualifies as pure, unadulterated babble.

Ablow's very convoluted multigenerational Freudian analysis of the Caylee Anthony case is a good example of why today's parents are having so much difficulty doing something that no generation who raised kids before the 1960s thought was difficult at all (despite the occasional bump in the road). But these foremothers and forefathers of ours never knew how lucky they were to have raised their children before mental health professionals began inventing complicated theories of child behavior and family dynamics.

My point is simply that the beat of parent-babble goes on. It has not slowed at all since the 1970s, and it has led parents down a long and winding road to nowhere. Somewhere during this aimless excursion, parents began asking why their children misbehaved. This was a new question. Our ancestors knew why children misbehaved; they were fundamentally self-centered and therefore inclined to do self-serving (wrong) things. Those supposedly unenlightened ancestors also understood that no matter how "good" a parent was by any standard, the parent's child was still capable of outrageous behavior.

The question "Why?" is nothing but a stumbling block for parents. After all, the answer is always speculative. It doesn't matter that the person giving the answer may be a well-known psychiatrist who often appears on television talk shows, the answer is still speculative—an educated guess. Capital letters after one's name do not mean one knows the answer; they only mean that one is able to construct a more complicated answer than less "educated" people are able to construct. But *complicated* and *correct* are not synonymous. Unfortunately, today's parents don't know that. So, thanks to people like Ablow, they come to believe in complicated explanations for their kids' misbehavior.

These complicated explanations always shift responsibility away from the child and induce "disciplinary paralysis" in parents. Unsure about who or what is responsible for the misbehavior—the child, themselves, or some complicated psychological mechanism—they don't know whom to correct. As a result, they hem and haw, try to understand, talk themselves blue in the face, and wind up doing nothing. So, the problem gets worse.

At some point, many of these parents seek help from someone representing the very profession that created much of the mess in the first place. All I have to say is, let the buyer beware.

NOTES

INTRODUCTION

xiv **Despite the fact that several of the most well-known:** Credible, objective research shows that human memory is language based, meaning that permanent memories do not form until language is well established—around the third birthday, on average. There is no evidence to suggest that memory of a traumatic event is an exception to this rule.

xvii **When I need advice concerning a problem in my life:** Researchers have found that when people do not know the academic qualifications of the therapist they are seeing, the clinical outcomes obtained by good-hearted people possessing nothing more than a high school education or a bachelor's degree unrelated to psychology, are basically equivalent to those obtained by good-hearted therapists with formal degrees in their field.

xix **Suddenly, the child and his or her supposed emotional needs:** It is convenient to blame Dr. Benjamin Spock, the author of what is widely concerned the first parenting book: *The Commonsense Book of Baby and Child Care* (1946). But Spock's view was originally very much in line with traditional child rearing. It was not until later that he was swept up in the psychological parenting revolution. Thus, it is not accurate to consider him one of its architects.

CHAPTER ONE: THE COST OF NEW IDEAS

7 **Since the 1950s, it is estimated that the suicide rate:** Statistics were obtained from an online article by Ernest J. Bordini, Ph.D., titled "Child and Adolescent Suicide," (2007). http://cpancf.com/articles_files/childadolescentsuicide.asp.

8 **And yet, amazingly, we did far better in school:** Snyder, T. (Ed.). (1993). *120 Years of American Education: A Statistical Portrait.* Excerpts taken from chapter one in *National Assessment of Adult Literacy (NAAL).* IES (Institute of Education Sciences), National Center for Education Statistics. http://nces.ed.gov/naal/lit_history.asp.

9 **In feelings:** Viscott, David. (2003). *Finding Your Strength in Difficult Times.* McGraw Hill; New York, New York, p. 195.

11 **Postmodernism postulates that many:** http://en.wikipedia.org/wiki/Postmodernism.

12 **More than half of today's kids will spend a significant portion:** See the official U.S. Census Web site (2010): http://census.gov/hhes/socdemo/marriage/data/cps/index.html.

21 **That goes a long way toward explaining:** Gutman, Myron P., Pullum-Pinon, Sara M., Pullum, Thomas W. (2002, Spring). "Three Eras of Young Adult Home Leaving in Twentieth Century America—1—Statistical Data Included." *Journal of Social History.* Vol. 35, No. 3.

CHAPTER TWO: AUTHORITY BABBLE

34 **In *Parent Effectiveness Training,* Gordon laments:** Gordon, Thomas (1970, 1975, 2000). *Parent Effectiveness Training: The Proven Program for Raising Responsible Children.* Three Rivers Press; New York, New York, p. 4.

35 **"As more people begin to understand power":** Ibid., p. 215.

36 **"These are adults who fill":** Ibid., pp. 206–207.

37 **To significant extent, his philosophy:** The children's rights movement has now become an international juggernaut that threatens the traditional right of American parents to exercise independent judgment in raising their children. I encourage readers to read a copy of the United Nations Convention on the Rights of the Child and to write letters to their U.S. senators in order to ensure that the U.S. Senate never ratifies the document.

37 **For example, Gordon asserted that "democratic relationships":** See Thomas Gordon's *Parent Effectiveness Training,* Preface, p. xiv.

41 **"Democratic families are peaceful families":** Ibid., Preface, p. xiv.

42 **Gordon even says:** Gordon, Thomas. (1989). *Teaching Children Self-Discipline at Home and at School.* Times Books; New York, New York, p. 239.

42 **"Always there is something going on":** See Thomas Gordon's *Parent Effectiveness Training,* p. 58.

44 **"Other parents find it difficult to throw":** Ibid., p. 320.

45 **"Why don't parents":** Ibid., p. 301.

45 **"It has impressed me to see":** Ibid., pp. 315–316.

46 **"Who is to decide what is in the best":** Ibid., p. 214.

50 **They negotiate conflict with their children:** Baumrind, Diana. (1966). "Effects of Authoritative Parental Control on Child Behavior." *Child Development,* Vol. 37, No. 4, pp. 887–907.

50 **Compared with children of either:** Baumrind, Diana. Ibid.

CHAPTER THREE: SELF-ESTEEM BABBLE

60 **In 1986, the governor:** The *New York Times* was just one of numerous newspapers and magazines that reported on Governor George Deukmejian's decision to sign into law legislation creating California's "State Task Force to Promote Self-Esteem and Personal and Social Responsibility." http://www.nytimes.com/1986/10/11/us/now-the-california-task-force-to-promote-self-esteem.html.

62 **Throughout the Bible:** The biblical references mentioned here are Proverbs 29:23 and Matthew 5:5.

63 **According to Maslow:** Maslow's beliefs about self-esteem were fully expressed as part of his "hierarchy of needs" in his 1954 book: Maslow, Abraham. (1954). *Motivation and Personality,* third edition. Harper and Row Publishers; New York, New York.

63 **He taught his students:** Carl Rogers expressed his belief in "unconditional positive regard"—the notion that therapists should suspend judgment and communicate unconditional acceptance and understanding—in such works as the following: Rogers, Carl. (1951). London: Constable. Rogers, Carl. (1959). "A Theory of Therapy, Personality and Interpersonal Relationships as Developed in the Client-Centered Framework." In (ed.) S. Koch, Vol. 3:. McGraw Hill; New York, New York.

63 **In 1969, in:** Branden, Nathaniel. (1969, 2001). *The Psychology of Self-Esteem*. Nash Publishing; Los Angeles, California (1969); and Jossey-Bass; San Francisco, California, p. 110.

65 **In it, Briggs taught that self-esteem:** Briggs, Dorothy Corkille. (1970). *Your Child's Self-Esteem: Step-by-Step Guidelines for Raising Responsible, Productive, Happy Children*. Double Day & Company, Inc.; New York, New York, pp. 2–3.

65 **These harmful self-beliefs:** Ibid., p. 35.

66 **In this way, parents annihilate:** Ibid., p. 183.

67 **The child supposedly:** Ibid., pp. 9–44.

70 **This is an unfortunate trend:** Blankenhorn, David. (1995). *Fatherless America: Confronting Our Most Urgent Social Problem*. Basic Books; New York, New York, pp. 9–25.

70 **At one point in her book:** Briggs, Dorothy Corkille. (1970). *Your Child's Self-Esteem: Step-by-Step Guidelines for Raising Responsible, Productive, Happy Children*. Double Day & Company, Inc.; New York, New York, p. 243.

72 **Baumeister, a former:** Bronson, Po. (2007). "How Not to Talk to Your Kids: The Inverse Power of Praise." Article accessed in May 2012 from the *New York Magazine* Web site, http://nymag.com/news/features/27840/.

73 **Most surprising is Baumeister's finding:** Baumeister, Roy F. and Boden, Joseph M. (1996). "Relation of Threatened Egotism to Violence and Aggression: The Dark Side of High Self-Esteem." *Psychological Review*, Vol. 103, No. 1, pp. 5–33. See also Baumeister, Roy. "Rethinking Self Esteem." *Stanford Social Innovation Review*. Winter 2005, which can be accessed at http://imaginefirestone.org/wp-content/uploads/2010/02/RethinkingSelf-Esteem.pdf.

73 **Baumeister and researcher Jean Twenge:** I am referring to Twenge's findings as reported by Lori Gottlieb in her 2011 article titled "How to Land Your Kid in Therapy," which appeared in *The Atlantic*, July/August 2011, pp. 64–78.

74 **According to the Brown Center:** Matthews, Jay. "For Math Students, Self Esteem Might Not Equal High Scores." *Washington Post.* October 18, 2006. This article is online at http://www.washingtonpost.com/wp-dyn/content/article/2006/10/17/AR2006101701298.html.

75 **On the other hand:** Stephenson, Frank. (2004). "For the Love of 'Me.'" Article accessed from the Florida State University Web site September 2004. http://www.research.fsu.edu/researchr/summer2004/coverstory.html.

75 **"What I think has gone wrong":** Stephenson, Frank. (2004). "For the Love of 'Me.'" 2004. Accessed in January 2012 from the Florida State University Web site, http://www.research.fsu.edu.

76 **They lack good coping skills:** Gottlieb, Lori. "How to Land Your Kid in Therapy." *The Atlantic,* July/August 2011, pp. 64–78.

78 **Interestingly enough:** Mueller, Claudia M. and Carol S. Dweck. (1998). "Praise for Intelligence Can Undermine Children's Motivation and Performance." *Journal of Personality and Social Psychology*, Vol. 75, No. 1, pp. 33–52.

78 **Baumeister has found that:** Bronson, Po. (2007). "How Not to Talk to Your Kids: The Inverse Power of Praise." Article accessed in May 2012 from the *New York Magazine* Web site, http://nymag.com/news/features/27840/.

78 **They actually value criticisms from teachers:** Ibid.

79 **In the final analysis, research:** Ibid.

CHAPTER FOUR: PUNISHMENT BABBLE

83 He also put: Ginott, Haim (2003). *Between Parent and Child: The Bestselling Classic That Revolutionized Parent-Child Communication (Revised and Updated)*. Three River Press. New York, New York

86 "The trouble with techniques that use": Ginnott, Haim. (1965, 2003). *Between Parent and Child*. Three Rivers Press; New York, New York.

88 "Because punishment, by definition": Gordon, Thomas. (1989). *Teaching Children Self-Discipline at Home and at School: New Ways Parents and Teachers Can Build Self-Control, Self-Esteem, and Self-Reliance*. Times Books; New York, New York, p. 231.

89 "Parents will want to communicate": See Thomas Gordon's *Parent Effectiveness Training*, p. 276.

91 We're both entitled to our own opinions: This oft-heard comment denies that one of the opinions being expressed is more correct than the other, or that one of the opinions may be flat-out wrong.

92 "In our training programs we try to help": See Thomas Gordon's *Teaching Children Self-Discipline at Home and at School*, pp. 106–107.

92 In *The Crime of Punishment:* Menninger, Karl. (2007 republished). *The Crime of Punishment*. Author House; Bloomington, Indiana.

93 Instead, Briggs insists that this toddler: See Dorothy Briggs's *Your Child's Self-Esteem*, pp. 187–188.

94 "The child who openly expresses": Ibid., p. 203.

97 Children are innocents: Ibid., pp. 130, 135, 150–151, 207.

CHAPTER FIVE: TOILET BABBLE

103 No single child-rearing task: A good amount of the material in this chapter has been taken from John Rosemond's previous book, *Toilet Training Without Tantrums*, Andrews McMeel (2012).

103 In the mid-1950s, for example: Sears, Robert, Eleanor Maccoby, and Harry Levin. (1958). *Patterns of Child Rearing*. Stanford University Press: California.

106 He said that regardless: Spock, Dr. Benjamin. (1946). *The Common-Sense Book of Baby and Child Care*. Pocket Books; New York, New York.

107 "If you want to be completely natural": Ibid.

108 "To continue to put diapers on a child": Ibid.

109 In this influential article: Brazelton, T. Berry. (1962, January). *Pediatrics*, Vol. 29, No. 1, pp 121–128.

110 **This overnight change in belief:** deVries, Marten W., and M. Rachel deVries. (1977, January). "Cultural Relativity of Toilet Training Readiness: A Perspective from East Africa." *Pediatrics*, Vol. 60, No. 2.

111 **Over the years, Brazelton has:** References to Dr. T. Berry Brazelton's toilet-training advice in this chapter were obtained from the following sources: *What Everybody Knows,* Addison-Wesley (1987). *Touchpoints: Your Child's Emotional and Behavioral Development,* Addison-Wesley (1992). *Toilet Training the Brazelton Way* (with Dr. Joshua Sparrow), DaCapo Press (2004). *Touchpoints Three to Six* (with Dr. Joshua Sparrow), Perseus Publishing (2001).

112 **On his Web site, pediatrician and author William Sears:** Dr. Sears's quote was obtained May 2012 from his Web site, http://www.askdrsears.com/topics/child-rearing-and-development/toilet-training/6-steps-d-day-diaper-free-day.

120 **In *The No-Cry Potty Training Solution*:** Pantley, Elizabeth. (2006). *The No-Cry Potty Training Solution.* McGraw-Hill; New York, New York.

CHAPTER SIX: ATTACHMENT BABBLE

127 **Attachment theory, first advanced:** Bowlby, J. (1951). "Maternal Care and Mental Health." World Health Organization Monograph.

128 **One of Bowlby's students:** Reference is made to Ainsworth's work in an online article by Dr. Doreen Arcus, Ph.D. University of Massachusetts Lowell http://findarticles.com/p/articles/mi_g2602/is_0000/ai_2602000016/ accessed July 2012, and is explained in detail by Dr. Ainsworth in her 1967 book: Ainsworth, Mary. (1967). *Infancy in Uganda: Infant Care and the Growth of Love.* John Hopkins Press, Baltimore, Oxford University Press, London, England

130 **The result is a baby:** Liedloff, Jean. (1975, 1977). *The Continuum Concept.* Perseus Books; Cambridge, Massassachusetts.

130 **In a 1998 interview, Liedloff:** Mendizza, Michael. (1998, Fall). "Allowing Human Nature to Work Successfully: A Very Candid Conversation with Jean Liedloff, Author of the *Continuum Concept.*" *Touch the Future.*

131 **Caretakers who respond:** See Liedloff, *The Continuum Concept.*

131 **Liedloff decried such Western childbirth:** Many experts believe that experiencing distress at separation from a mother or primary caregiver is an essential part of teaching children to self-pacify and to feel secure, knowing that parents will return. There is no scientific evidence that parents who allow their children to experience periods of controlled "separation anxiety" are harming their children. Items like playpens,

when used wisely and sparingly to confine a child for his or her own protection while a parent is temporarily unable to provide supervision, are not shown to cause any harm to a child's development.

132 **In the 1970s and 1980s:** Bradshaw, John. (1988, 2005). *Healing the Shame That Binds You*. Health Communications, Inc.; Deerfield Beach, Florida.

134 **According to Thevenin:** Thevenin, Tine. (1987). *The Family Bed: An Age Old Concept in Child Rearing*. Avery Publishing Group; Wayne, New Jersey, pp. 66–67.

135 **Common sense says that:** There is nothing wrong with an infant sleeping in a bassinet or crib that is located in the parents' bedroom. However, said crib should be moved to the child's own room once the child begins sleeping through the night or when he or she turns six months, whichever comes first.

138 **He goes on to promise parents:** Sears, William and Martha Sears. (2001). *The Attachment Parenting Book*. Little, Brown, and Company; New York, New York, pp. 5–6.

139 **On his Web site, in an essay:** Sears, William. "11 Ways to Raise a Truthful Child." Accessed July 2012. http://www.askdrsears.com/topics/discipline-behavior/morals-manners/11-ways-raise-truthful-child.

139 **This is pure, unadulterated hogwash:** The senior Dr. Sears is not the only member of the Sears family guilty of selling unsubstantiated claims to a mass audience. In 2007, one of Sears's sons—also a doctor and a product of the very attachment parenting methods Dr. Sears claims will produce more honest children who "don't need to lie"—published what became a best-seller: *The Vaccine Book*. In it, the younger Dr. Sears presents a schedule by which parents can delay, space out, or withhold vaccines. As it turns out, Dr. Sears's schedule runs counter to recommendations by the American Academy of Pediatrics, the Centers for Disease Control, and the American Academy of Family Physicians. Following scathing critiques from such noted physicians as Dr. Paul Offit, who wrote a blistering indictment of Sears's claims in the January 2009 issue of *Pediatrics*, and Dr. Seth Mnookin, who lectures at MIT and who called *The Vaccine Book* a collection of "obfuscation and misinformation," the younger Dr. Sears has since backed away from his profitable antivaccine pandering.

140 **Mom will know that she has connected:** See Dr. Sears's *The Attachment Parenting Book*, p. 82.

141 **On his Web site:** Accessed from Dr. William Sears's Web site May 2012, http://www.askdrsears.com/topics/attachment-parenting/attachment-research. In an online article at http://www.aboutkidshealth.ca/en/

news/series/attachment/pages/attachment-part-four-parent-and-child-influences-on-attachment.aspx, psychologist Dr. Susan Goldberg cites this same study, commenting that "Researchers have since tried to replicate these findings with mixed results." In other words, the results are unreliable, therefore, fairly worthless.

145 **Research finds:** Information accessed from the U.S. Library of Medicine's Web site, July 2012, http://www.ncbi.nlm.nih.gov/pubmedhealth/PMH0002533/ and are supported, in part, by the findings of the Task Force on Sudden Infant Death Syndrome. "The Changing Concept of Sudden Infant Death Syndrome: Diagnostic Coding Shifts, Controversies Regarding the Sleeping Environment, and New Variables to Consider in Reducing Risk." (2005), . Nov; 116, p. 5.

146 **When babies sleep in the same rooms:** Among many other studies, research confirming these general trends are found in the following: Sadeh, "Assessment and Intervention for Infant Night Waking: Parental Reports and Activity-Based Home Monitoring," *Journal of Consulting and Clinical Psychology*, Vol. 62, p. 63. Mosko, Richard and McKenna, "Infant Arousals During Mother-Infant Bed Sharing: Implications for Infant Sleep and Sudden Infant Death Syndrome Research," (1997), *Pediatrics,* Vol. 100, p. 841. First Candle Web site: http://www.firstcandle.org/new-expectant-parents/bedtime-basics-for-babies/room-sharing-makes-breastfeeding-easier/, accessed July 2012.

146 **He also claims to have found:** McKenna, James J. (May 2012). http://cosleeping.nd.edu/controversies/in-response-to-john-rosemond/.

146 **He even suggests it was immoral for the AAP:** McKenna, James J. "Co-Sleeping and Biological Imperatives: Why Human Babies Do Not and Should Not Sleep Alone." http://www.naturalchild.org/james_mckenna/biological.html (date of posting not given).

146 **A 2012 meta-analysis of eleven controlled studies:** Moyer, Melinda Wenner. *Slate.* http://www.slate.com/articles/health_and_science/medical_examiner/2012/03/mayim_bialik_s_beyond_the_sling_doesn_t_give_all_the_facts_on_bed_sharing.html. March 8, 2012.

147 **She admits that she:** Bialik, Mayim. (2012). *Beyond the Sling: A Real-Life Guide to Raising Confident, Loving Children the Attachment Parenting Way.* Touchstone; New York, New York.

147 **Nevertheless, she goes on to praise:** Ibid.

147 **McKenna also says that the benefits of co-sleeping:** James J. McKenna, Ph.D. (May 2012) http://cosleeping.nd.edu/controversies/in-response-to-john-rosemond/.

148 **The variables measured included social skills:** http://www.eurekalert.org/ pub_releases/2002-08/cfta-cah080702.php.

148 **Callahan writes that:** Quote accessed from Dr. Callaway's blog, May 2012: http://scienceofmom.com.

150 **In that regard, developmental psychologist Burton White:** Dr. White reported this research-based finding during a presentation he gave in Raleigh, North Carolina, in 1978. The author was in the audience.

151 **"There is no way to get a child":** Ms. Rihani's comment regarding Dr. William Sears's *The Attachment Parenting Book* was obtained in May 2012 from book reviews posted by readers on Amazon.com, http://www.amazon.com/Attachment-Parenting-Book-Commonsense-Understanding/product-reviews.

154 **Insufficient sleep:** In addition to numerous sources, the effects of insufficient sleep are documented in a report on the Harvard medical school Web site: "Consequences of Insufficient Sleep." http://healthysleep. med.harvard.edu/healthy/matters/consequences. Accessed July 2012.

154 **There is obvious benefit to a marriage:** While it is true that good, objectionable research concludes that, on average, children benefit significantly from growing up in two-parent households, it is also true that single parents can certainly do a good job of raising emotionally healthy children.

CHAPTER SEVEN: ADOPTION BABBLE

158 **Oh, and they "grieve":** A close relationship exists between attachment-parenting "babble" and adoption "babble."

169 **In the 1950s, Dr. John Bowlby's research:** Bowlby, J. (1950, 1995), *Maternal Care and Mental Health*, the master work series (second edition), Northvale, New Jersey; Jason Aronson (Geneva, World Health Organization, monograph series no. 3), London; and Bowlby, J. (1969, 1999), *Attachment. Attachment and Loss* (volume one, second edition), Basic Books, New York.

169 **According to the *Diagnostic and Statistical*:** Data taken from the *Diagnostic and Statistical Manual for Mental Disorders* (*DSM*)-IV-TR (2000). American Psychiatric Association, p. 129.

170 **Experts say that RAD:** Ibid., p. 129.

174 **Without empirical evidence:** By elevating an unsubstantiated observation to the level of social theory, it provided mental health professionals yet another opportunity to latch onto a new, unproven theory from which they could, yet again, create a market for themselves.

174 **"There is no doubt that adopters":** Dr. Kirk's quote was obtained from an excerpt from his book *A Theory of Adoption and Mental Health* (1964), as accessed in May 2012 from the Web site for the Adoption History Project, http://darkwing.uoregon.edu/~adoption/archive/KirkSF.htm.

175 **In a 2010 article, adoption specialist:** Vivo, Meghan. "About Reactive Attachment Disorder." Accessed May 2012 from the Adoption Information Resource Center Web site, http://www.adoptionissues.org/adoption/about-reactive-attachment-disorder.htm.

176 **For example, Mayo claims:** Information accredited to the Mayo Clinic was obtained in May 2012 from the Mayo Clinic Web site, http://www.mayoclinic.com/health/reactive-attachment-disorder/DS00988.

177 **An implicit lack:** *Diagnostic and Statistical Manual for Mental Disorders* (DSM)-IV-TR (2000). American Psychiatric Association, p. 129.

177 **Even kids who experience abrupt:** Prior, V. and Glaser, D. (2006). *Understanding Attachment and Attachment Disorders.* Jessica Kingsley Publishers; London, United Kingdom, pp. 218–219.

178 **They adjusted well, overcame the trauma:** Goldfarb, W. (1955). "Emotional and Intellectual Consequences of Psychologic Deprivation in Infancy: A Re-evaluation." P. Hoch and J. Zubin (Eds.). *Psychopathology of Childhood.* Grune & Stratton; New York, New York, pp. 105–19.

178 **More recent research shows:** Rutter, M. (2002). "Nature, Nurture, and Development: From Evangelism Through Science Toward Policy and Practice." *Child Development,* Vol. 73, No. 1, pp. 1–21.

178 **"There is also a substantial body":** Bruer, John T. (1999). *The Myth of the First Three Years.* The Free Press; New York, New York, p. 53.

178 **After being adopted:** Bruer, John T. (1999). *The Myth of the First Three Years.* The Free Press; New York, New York, pp. 106–143. Bruer's research and similar findings from other research are nicely reviewed in an online piece from *The New Yorker* magazine at http://www.gladwell.com/2000/2000_01_10_a_baby.html.

178 **Research has shown that:** Feigelman, W. (1997). "Comparisons with Persons Raised in Conventional Families." *Marriage & Family Review,* 1540–9635, Vol. 25, No. 3, pp. 199–223.

179 **"We [adoptive parents] don't need":** Melina, Lois R. (1986). *Raising Adopted Children: A Manual for Adoptive Parents.* Solstice Press; New York, New York, p. 51.

179 **One of the best studies of the long-term effect:** Bohman, M., and Sigvardsson, S. (1990). "Outcome in Adoption: Lessons from Longitudinal Studies." In David M. Brodzinsky and Marshall D.

Schechter (Eds.). *The Psychology of Adoption*. Oxford University Press; New York, New York, pp. 93–106.

CHAPTER EIGHT: SPANKING BABBLE

190 **When Straus's research design is applied:** Larzelere, Robert E. and Baumrind, Diana. (2010). "Are Spanking Injunctions Scientifically Supported?" p. 79. This article was obtained in May 2012 from Duke University's law library Web site, http://www.law.duke.edu/journals/lcp.

190 **Whenever another researcher:** Taken from notes made during a phone conversation with Dr. Larzelere in April 2012.

190 **Larzelere has also discovered:** Larzelere, Robert E. and Baumrind, Diana. (2010). "Are Spanking Injunctions Scientifically Supported?" This article was obtained in May 2012 from Duke University's law library Web site, http://www.law.duke.edu/journals/lcp.

191 **Ten years later, Larzelere found:** Larzelere, Robert E. and Johnson, Byron. (1999). "Evaluations of the Effects of Sweden's Spanking Ban on Physical Child Abuse Rates: A Literature Review." *Psychological Reports*. Vol. 85, pp. 381–392.

191 **Baumrind concludes that:** Baumrind, D. (1973). "The Development of Instrumental Competence through Socialization." In A. D. Pick (Ed.), *Minnesota Symposia on Child Psychology*, Vol. 7, pp. 3–46. University of Minnesota Press; Minneapolis, Minnesota. Also Baumrind, Diana. (1966). "Effects of Authoritative Parental Control on Child Behavior." *Child Development*. Vol. 37, No. 4, pp. 887–907.

192 **Fuller also discovered that:** Kettle, Theodore. "Pro-Spanking Studies May Have Global Effect." (2010). Article was accessed May 2012 from the Newsmax Web site, http://www.newsmax.com/US/spanking-studies-children-spock/2010/01/07/id/345669.

192 **Gunnoe concluded:** Ibid.

192 **She also found that:** Ibid.

193 **"Even the most clinically defiant":** Larzelere, Robert E. and Baumrind, Diana. (2010). "Are Spanking Injunctions Scientifically Supported?" This article was obtained in May 2012 from Duke University's law library Web site, http://www.law.duke.edu/journals/lcp.

195 **"I think it's pretty hard to argue":** Zapler, Mike. "No-spank bill on way." January 19, 2007. Obtained from the Web site Infowars.com, http://www.infowars.com/articles/ps/spanking_no_spanking_bill_on_way_california.htm.

195 **On DrSpock.com:** Kettle, Theodore. "Pro-Spanking Studies May Have Global Effect," January 2010. http://www.newsmax.com/US/spanking-studies-children-spock/2010/01/07/id/345669. Accessed July 2012.

195 **In the first edition (1946):** Spock, Benjamin. (1946). *The Common-Sense Book of Baby and Child Care.* Penguin Group; New York, New York.

195 **It is nothing short of naive:** See Kettle's article on newsmax.com, "Pro-Spanking Studies May Have Global Effect."

195 **The American Academy of Pediatrics':** See the American Academy of Pediatrics Guidance for Effective Discipline. http://pediatrics.aappublications.org/content/101/4/723.long.

196 **For example, Holden asserts:** Holden, George W. "Proposal for a Resolution to be Endorsed by the Society for Research in Human Development." February 2, 2011. This document was sent to me by Dr. Robert Larzelere.

196 **In his SRHD proposal, Holden:** Ibid.

197 **Holden goes on to say that spanking:** Ibid.

197 **Larzelere writes, "I do not doubt":** Larzelere's quote and the account of his attempt to engage George Holden in dialogue are taken from a document Larzelere authored in March 2012 titled "Scientific Evidence For and Against Advocacy Resolutions Should be Fully Considered Before Scientific Societies Endorse Advocacy Resolutions: The Case of Supporting Spanking Bans."

201 **Of the three groups, their kids:** See Baumrind's 1966 article, "Effects of Authoritative Parental Control on Child Behavior."

202 **Spankings are most effective:** Larzelere, Robert E. and Baumrind, Diana, ibid.

CHAPTER NINE: THE BEAT GOES ON

207 **Whether Casey was directly responsible:** Albow, Keith. (2011). *Inside the Mind of Casey Anthony: A Psychological Portrait.* St. Martin's Press; New York, New York.